KNITTING TIPS & TRADE SECRETS

EXPANDED

KNITTING TIPS & TRADE SECRETS

EXPANDED

Ingenious Techniques and Solutions for
Hand and Machine Knitting and Crochet

The Taunton Press

The Taunton Press

The Taunton Press, Inc., 63 South Main Street,
PO Box 5506, Newtown, CT 06470-5506
e-mail: tp@taunton.com

Editor: Pam Hoenig
Jacket/Cover/Interior design and layout: Sonia Shannon

Library of Congress Cataloging-in-Publication Data

Knitting tips & trade secrets expanded : ingenious techniques and solutions for hand
and machine knitting and crochet / [editor, Pam Hoenig].
     p. cm.
  Includes index.
  ISBN-13: 978-1-56158-871-8
  ISBN-10: 1-56158-871-7
  1. Knitting. 2. Machine knitting. 3. Crocheting. I. Hoenig, Pam. II. Title: Knitting tips
and trade secrets expanded.
  TT820.K7255 2006
  746.43'2--dc22
                                    2006015929

Printed in the United States of America

10 9 8 7 6 5 4 3 2 1

The following manufacturers/names appearing in *Knitting Tips & Trade Secrets Expanded*
are trademarks: Boye®, Fray Check™, Macintosh®, MacDraft®, NeedleMaster™,
Post-it® Note, Scotch®, Static Guard®, Superba®, Velcro®, Wrights®

CONTENTS

Yarn 2

Hand-Knitting Techniques 18

Multicolor Knitting 62

Garment-Making Tips 82

Managing Your Knitting 118

Machine Knitting 136

Crochet Tips 146

Finishing and Caring for Your Project 160

Knitting abbreviations 182

Index 183

ONE

YARN

Types of Yarn

How Much Is Enough?

Winding Yarn

Yarn Holders

Yarn Stash

Recycling Yarn

Odds and Ends

TYPES OF YARN

Know your chenille

In my experience, some chenilles, when knit, will "ratchet" themselves out of the knitted stitches. After putting a lot of money into the yarn and hours into knitting, I found that upon the first wearing of the chenille sweaters, loops appeared wherever the knitted fabric was stretched. As I understand from at least one yarn supplier, some chenilles are not recommended for knitting, so it's always a good idea to ask about use before you buy.

— *Dana Sagar, Warrenton, VA*

Knitting to gauge in acrylics

There's almost no comparison between wool and acrylic as knitting yarns. If you're determined to knit with acrylic yarn, be sure to use a major brand. All acrylics are not created equal, and you definitely get what you pay for. Some simply feel better than others, and the better brands will have more body and be much less stretchy. If you're an experienced wool knitter, the biggest surprise you'll encounter is that you can't change the shape or size of acrylic knits by blocking, so your gauge accuracy is doubly important.

Here's my method for knitting a gauge swatch: I cast on 20 or 22 stitches and knit a few rows in garter stitch, after which I knit in pattern for 16 to 18 rows, adding garter-stitch selvages. Then I switch to the next largest needles, knit a few more garter-stitch rows, and repeat. I'll use three or sometimes four sizes of needles on one swatch.

After finishing the swatch—and this is crucial—I wash and dry it just as I plan to wash and dry the finished garment. For acrylic, I throw it into the washer and dryer, which can change its texture and appearance considerably.

Then I simply pick the most attractive section of the swatch (or I use it to determine which size needles I should start with on the next swatch) and figure out its stitch and row counts. I don't necessarily try to match the gauge of the pattern. If I like that particular yarn and stitch pattern the way I knit it at 8 stitches per inch but the pattern calls for

6 stitches per inch, I convert the pattern to my preferred gauge with a bit of easy proportional mathematics: If the pattern calls for a cast-on of 100 stitches at 6 stitches per inch, I convert it to the same length at 8 stitches per inch. I do this by multiplying 100 by 8, then dividing 800 by 6 to get 133.33 stitches, which I round off to 133. Row counts can be converted in the same way.
— *Dorothy Ratigan*

Knitting with alpaca yarns

Because alpaca lacks crimp, alpaca yarns do not bounce back the way wool yarns do. In fact, alpaca yarns hang limply, as do many silk, angora, cotton, and linen yarns. To make sure your finished sweater won't stretch, knit and finish generous swatches by hand or machine. Launder, block, dry, and finish the swatches the same way the final garment will be handled. If the item is to be dry cleaned, don't launder the sample; steam (don't press) it to release any distortion. Measure the swatches carefully and use exact stitch gauge.

In designing alpaca knits, here are some things to consider: The fiber is very warm, so even light, lacy knits are quite toasty. When you make knit garments with sleeves (particularly lacy ones), you need to reinforce the shoulder seams to prevent the weight of the sleeves from stretching them. I either hand-stitch narrow satin ribbon across the shoulder seams as a stabilizer—going across the back neck edge as well, if the design permits—or I seam the shoulder firmly with backstitch. I avoid grafted seams at the shoulder in sleeved garments.

Alpaca yarns (commercial or handspun), with their soft, silky, slippery texture, can cause hand and machine knitters a bit of grief because they tend to split easily. Cabled yarns, which are twisted together, or two or more two-ply yarns are less likely to split than plain plied yarns. But the more twist yarns have in both the single and plied states, the less soft and lofty the finished knitting will be. You'll also have more trouble with splitting if you knit tightly. Try using a smaller needle size and maintaining a looser tension to alleviate the problem. To help cope with splitting, I knit with needles of a color that contrasts with the yarn, use a strong light, and try to knit when distractions are few.

Alpaca yarns work well for machine knitters. I have used several commercial and handspun yarns on a variety of knitting machines with very little difficulty. Of course, if the machine tension is too great, yarn breaks will occur, and if the tension is too little, dropped or split stitches will result. The only problem I have encountered is that commercially dyed yarns tend to break in lace patterns. I don't have this problem with my handspun, hand-dyed alpaca yarn.

— *Julie Owen*

Experiment with variegated yarns for the best results

A variegated yarn changes colors along its length. The colors can be the result of blending, dyeing, or printing. An advantage to knitting with a variegated yarn is that you can change colors without switching yarns, thus avoiding yarn ends. Often the colors in variegated yarn appear sequentially at regular intervals on the strand. When knitting a narrow area with such yarn, the colors may shade gradually from one to the next. By contrast, in a wide section, the colors may appear jumbled, like in a tweed. You can experiment on swatches to explore the options for different effects.

Two variegated balls are better than one

Variegated yarns knit up in patches of color instead of in the soft, heathery look the skeins had. And the design of the patches can change drastically when you knit a sleeve or cardigan front, for example, because of the change in the width of the knitting. To minimize the patching, knit two rows from one ball of yarn, then two rows from another, then two rows from the first, and so on. You'll have short yarn floats at the edge, but the colors will be more evenly distributed.

— *Ruth Galpin, Southport, CT*

HOW MUCH IS ENOUGH?

Don't come up short midrow

If the yarn you have left is four times the width of the knitting, you'll have enough to knit one more row.

— *Bea Stone, Chestnut Hill, MA*

A tale of two skeins

If you have only one remaining skein of yarn, how do you tell if there is enough yarn left to knit any pairs of extras (such as sleeve trims) on a sweater? If you divide the one skein into two equal balls, it is easier to tell. To divide the skein, wind a ball from each end without cutting the yarn. Weigh the balls separately, winding and rewinding until they have the same yardage. Now cut them apart.

— *Liz Violante, Marco Island, FL*

Calculating what you need with sport-weight and fingering yarns

Sport-weight yarn contains from 1,200 to 1,700 yards per pound, or 130 to 185 yards per 50-gram ball, and knits to a gauge of about 6 stitches per inch on size 4 to 6 needles.

Fingering- or baby-weight yarn is thinner and gives a finer gauge (more stitches and rows per inch), with 1,700 to 2,800 yards per pound, or 185 to 300 yards per 50-gram ball. Knitting fingering-weight yarn with size 2 to 4 needles gives a gauge of around 7 stitches per inch, depending on the yarn, the fiber content, and the tension at which it's knit.

How to measure yarn yardage

I know a remarkably simple way to estimate how many yards per pound your yarns contain. You can make an easy yarn balance from inexpensive, readily available materials—a soda can, a spring-type clothespin, a plastic soda straw, two paper cups, string, tape, a long straight pin, and some paper clips. With this contraption, based on the soda-can balance developed by Ron Marson of Canby, Oregon, for use in science classes, you can weigh a yard of your yarn and quickly estimate the number of yards per pound. To make the balance, bend the pop-top ring on the soda can straight up and clip the clothespin onto it. Stick a folded strip of tape onto each clothespin arm and cut a U-shaped notch in each folded edge of tape. Insert the straight pin into the center of the plastic straw and balance the pin in the two tape notches of the clothespin.

Next, thread a piece of string through the straw and tie a paper clip on each end of the string near the straw. Tape another piece of string across the center of each paper cup and hang a cup from the paper clip at each end of the straw. If the cups aren't level when empty, adjust the balance by adding pieces of tape to the straw on the higher side until the cups are level.

You'll use whole and cut pieces of standard No. 1 paper clips and weights to balance a length of your yarn. Each clip is about 4 inches long when straightened and weighs about .5 gram. Use a fine-point felt-tip pen and wire cutters to mark and cut a straightened clip in half; then mark and cut one half into quarters, and a quarter into eighths, and an eighth into sixteenths.

Now for the easy part—using the balance: Put a 1-yard piece of yarn in one of the cups. Place paper-clip pieces in the other cup until the two cups balance as closely as possible, then count the number of clips you used. Add the cut clip pieces as fractions (for example, ¼ is .25, ⅛ is .125, etc.). Finally, divide 900 by the number of clips. The result is the number of yards in a pound of that yarn.

For more accuracy with a lightweight yarn, you might want to weigh 2 or 3 yards of yarn, in which case you'll divide the number of clips into 1,800 or 2,700, respectively. For a yard of cotton yarn I recently weighed, I found that ½ plus ¹⁄₁₆ clip was a little too heavy, and ½ clip alone was a little too light, so I split the difference and used ½ plus ¹⁄₃₂ (.5312). Dividing 900 by .5312 gave 1,694 yards per pound, which is quite close to the package label of 1,689 yards per pound.

It's amazing that this simple balance is accurate to .05 grams! The only drawback is that this little balance can't measure things too weighty for the soda-straw balance beam. Maybe someone out there can improve on the design to solve this problem.

— *Tina Bradford*

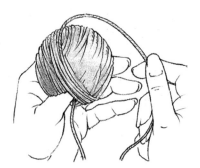

Fig. 1

Leaving a tail, wind yarn around left thumb at a 45° angle, rotating ball to keep wraps even.

WINDING YARN

Making a center-pull ball

I prefer to wind my skeined yarn by hand rather than use a mechanical ball winder, even though it takes longer, because it allows me to become acquainted with the yarn before I knit with it. When the skein is open and untied (you can put it on the back of a chair, on your knees, or in someone else's hands), pinch the tail between your left thumb and forefinger, about a foot from the end. Then, with your left thumb as a pivot, wrap the yarn around it at about a 45° angle *(see Fig. 1)*. Use your left forefinger to move the ball clockwise around your thumb as you wind onto it, keeping the same angle as you wrap the yarn. Be careful not to stretch the yarn, or it will lose its loft. Just guide it from the skein onto your thumb fairly loosely, being careful not to twist it.

If you continue to wind the yarn uniformly like this, you'll finish with a nicely wound ball that's flat on the top and bottom so it will sit in your basket or on the floor without rolling. When you get to the end of the skein, tuck it under several layers of wrapped yarn on the ball. Remove the ball from your thumb and pull the yarn easily from the center, where your thumb used to be.

— *Cathy Collier, Ashland, OR*

Another way to wind a center-pull ball

To make a foolproof yarn ball that pulls from the center without tangling, start with a plastic medicine bottle. Place the end of the yarn inside the bottle and snap the cap in place. Wind the yarn loosely around the bottle, keeping the cap above the edge of the ball *(see Fig. 2)*. When all is wound, remove the bottle, release the yarn end, and you have a center-pull ball that won't roll away.

— *Lois Carroll, Parma, OH*

Fig. 2

The magic of a roll-proof ball

After many years of having balls of yarn rolling around and hiding under chairs, I received this super tip from a blind friend. Leave about a 5-inch tail when you start wrapping the yarn around your fingers. Wrap as you would any ball, always leaving the tail free. Tuck the other end of the yarn under a strand when you're done. The yarn pulls from the center, and the ball stays put.
— *Esther Rumaner, North Fort Myers, FL*

Make squishy yarn balls

Winding your yarn ball too tightly can make a difference in your knitting or weaving. When the stretched yarn relaxes, the gauge of your piece changes. To avoid stretching the yarn when you wind, make the first few wraps around your fingers to form the core of the ball. Instead of taking your fingers out of the way of your winding on successive layers, wind the yarn over them. Slip your fingers out and wind the next layer over them. This way you add slack to each layer in the ball, and the yarn doesn't stretch.

If you're using a ball or cone winder and a swift, keep the swift moving a little faster than you're drawing the yarn into the ball or cone. Do this by giving the swift a gentle push to keep some slack in the yarn as it feeds onto the winder. These methods may give you squishy yarn balls, but the yarn will be its own natural size.
— *Carol Hillestad, Cresco, PA*

Keeping it loose

When I wind yarn skeins into balls for knitting, I wrap the yarn around four fingers. I slide my fingers out every six wraps to vary the direction of the winding. Then I continue, still winding the yarn around all four fingers and the ball. I get a nice loose ball, and my yarn is never stretched from being wound too tightly.
— *Dorothy Collins, Buffalo, NY*

YARN HOLDERS
Great yarn holder

Empty baby-wipe containers with flip-up tops make great yarn holders for knitting. Just cut away the center of the lid, place the skein in the container, and pull the yarn up

Fig. 3

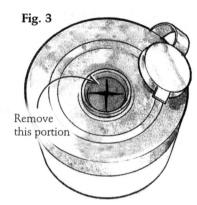

Remove
this portion

Baby-wipe container

through the hole *(see Fig. 3)*. When you're not knitting, the sealing tab holds the yarn so it doesn't pull out.

— *Darlene McNamara, Willowdale,*
ON, Canada

Yarn control

Plastic soda bottles make great yarn caddies for pull-skein yarn. Simply cut a generous hole in the side of a clean soda bottle, slip the skein in, and thread the end through the bottle neck. Two-liter bottles will hold a large 4-ounce skein, and 1-liter bottles work well for 1- or 2-ounce skeins.

— *Carol Carvalho, Malibu, CA*

Knitters need baggies!

After winding yarn into a ball on my ball winder, I slip it into a sandwich bag and fold over the built-in flap. I put the yarn wrapper or some other identification in the bag so I will remember what the yarn is. When I am ready to knit, I punch a hole in the bag and retrieve the center end of the skein. The plastic bag not only keeps the yarn clean but holds the skein together and prevents

the yarn from tangling. The yarn flows from the skein smoothly when I am knitting by machine. The uniform, labeled skeins also stack and store nicely.

— *Melissa Yoder, Durham, NC*

Taming slippery yarn balls

To keep balls of yarn from unraveling while you're knitting, put them in a pouch made from the foot of an old stocking. To make the pouch, cut the foot off midway and make a drawstring by threading waste yarn in and out of the cut edge. Pop the yarn into the pouch, leaving an end hanging out, and pull the drawstring to close the bag. Support hose seems to work especially well.

— *Barbara Eckman, Chicago, IL*

Managing ribbon yarn

When I'm using ribbon yarn, I make a small slit in the lid of a box that fits the ribbon spool and then thread the ribbon through the slit. The spool stays put, and the ribbon won't twist.

— *Avis Irey, Melvern, KS*

Coping with elastic thread

With all the lovely but inelastic cotton yarns available today, many people are knitting elastic threads into their ribbings along with the yarn. Unfortunately, the spools of elastic can be difficult to manage. I put a large hardbound book on the seat next to me, with the spine against my leg, and lay the spool on its side next to the front edge of the book, with the thread winding off the top of the spool. This setup prevents the spool from rolling around and allows the thread to pay out without tangling.

— *Helen Ettinger, Northbrook, IL*

Cone holders for knitters

My husband built me a little stand to help with knitting from cones. He drilled two holes in a 7-inch-square block of wood. He set a 4-inch dowel in the center hole to hold the cone and a 36-inch dowel with a cup hook near the top in the corner hole, as shown in *Fig. 4*. The yarn feeds smoothly into my hands without jerking and pulling.

— *Joan Debolt, Bradford, PA*

YARN STASH
Storing your yarn collection

I've never been able to pass up yarn sales. The result: dozens of skeins just waiting for the right project to come along. To keep my yarn in order, as well as dust and moth free, I store it in multilevel hanging sweater bags with clear vinyl fronts. Pop a cedar wood block on every level, and you're set. I use two bags: one for fingering through worsted weight and another for bulky weight.

— *Susan Redlich, Natrona Heights, PA*

Keeping tabs on your stash

I buy lots of yarn wherever I go, and I keep it protected from moths in a huge storage box under a built-in couch. The problem was how to remember what I had without digging through the whole collection. My solution was to take a heavy piece of paper and staple on the yarn label with a yarn sample around it. Next to it I write how many balls I have, where and when it was bought, price, probable use, tension, and

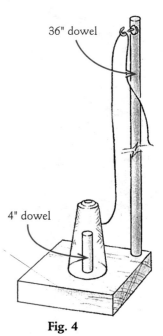

36" dowel

4" dowel

Fig. 4

needle size. Two of these sheets put my yarn supply at hand at a moment's notice. You could also put the information on index cards.

— *Marion Poller, Herzliya, Israel*

Got an old aquarium?

I finally found a good use for an old glass aquarium we had in the garage. I cleaned it thoroughly, hauled it into my knitting area, and then filled it with my leftover yarns. It's convenient, mothproof, and very pretty!

— *Nadine Skotheim, San Marino, CA*

Visible yarn storage

Some yarns are too beautiful to be tucked away in a basket or cubbyhole. To get them out where you can enjoy them, hang them on fish stringers—the kind with a chain and snap hooks *(see Fig. 5)*. I hang the stringers from a rafter, up against my studio wall. Each snap hook will take two or three skeins, hung from a tie. And, since they're out in the light and air, insects are less attracted to them.

—*Sharon Lappin Lumsden, Champaign, IL*

Fig. 5

Marking yarn-ball ends

Avid hand knitters tend to acquire lots of yarn balls of odds and ends, which often unravel easily or have hard-to-find ends. To avoid a mess, I secure and mark the yarn ends with a fine metal hairpin tied at the bend with a piece of contrasting yarn. Insert the pin over the tail and into the ball. When you use that yarn again, the end will easily be found!

— *Sue Johnson, Sagle, ID*

Make your own designer yarns

If you have sufficient leftover yarn and thread stashes, you can create new yarns by twisting them together. Combined yarns produce tweedy, colorful textures in sweaters and vests. For a "strawberries and cream" designer yarn, I wind together one strand each of yellow baby yarn; tatting thread in solid white, pink, and yellow; and variegated yellow and pink tatting threads.

If you don't have fine leftover threads or yarns, consider garage sales and second-hand shops, or buy someone else's yarn odds and ends.

— *Sylvia Landman, Novato, CA*

RECYCLING YARN

High-quality wool yarn doesn't have to be costly

There's only one drawback to being a regular knitter, if you discount ignoring one's spouse, children, and work. Knitting begins to get expensive after a while because good yarn isn't cheap. I'm sure that one reason so many people get into spinning is so they have a ready source of inexpensive yarn. But there's another yarn source close at hand that's cheaper and less time-consuming than spinning. I'm talking about reusing the yarn from old sweaters.

I've found that yard sales, rummage sales, and flea markets are the best sources for cheap yarn. At one recent flea market I went to, for example, I found men's sweaters for 25¢ each. If you decide to go this route, however, there are a couple of things to watch for. One thing to check is the texture of the sweater. If the sweater is very fuzzy and has become severely matted with heavy use, it will be difficult to unravel. It's also important to look at the seams.

Cheap sweaters are often cut and seamed out of whole knitted cloth, just the way other garments are made. This means that if you try to unravel the sweater, you will end up with a lot short pieces. Better-quality sweaters are knit of a continuous strand of yarn, so the seams inside will have finished, turned edges at the ends of the rows. That's the kind to look for; imported sweaters are more likely to be knitted that way. If the colors aren't just right, don't worry. Many imported handknit sweaters are made of natural wool that can be dyed.

The last step before converting your sweaters into yarn is the unraveling. Pick apart the seams, being careful to cut only the strand of yarn that was used to sew the sweater pieces together. Find the end of the yarn where it is woven into the fabric, draw it out, and begin unraveling. The cast-off row at the edge of the knitting is tenacious, and ribbing is a little stiffer to unravel than straight stitch. But these are minor problems.

As you unravel, wind the yarn into balls of convenient size. There usually is a break at a good place to suggest the start of a new ball. The yarn has a kinkiness from being knit up so long, which I like in the new garments.

But I have noticed that when reclaimed yarn is wound tightly in a ball and has been kept for a while, the kinks subside and the yarn straightens out.

You'd be surprised at how fast you will collect an interesting assortment of fine wool, and you'll be pleased to discover how being an avid and creative knitter need not be expensive.

— *Bruce Bush, Mount Rainier, MD*

Fresh wool from recycled sweaters

Unraveled yarn from old handknit sweaters comes out looking, and knitting, like brand new wool if you loosely wrap it into skeins, tie each skein in four places, then soak the skeins in warm soapy water, agitating as little as possible. Rinse thoroughly and hang the skeins to dry before balling. Some of my treasured wools have been knitted into sweaters as many as three times and still look and feel great.

— *Helen Benninger, Willowdale, ONT, Canada*

Another method for recycling sweater yarn

I have been recycling sweaters that I knitted by hand or purchased ever since I can remember. I wind the yarn into skeins (across the back of a chair, for example) and then soak the skeins in warm water overnight.

The next morning I retrieve the soaking skeins carefully without squeezing them at all, then thread them onto a broomstick and hang the broomstick parallel to the floor. I then thread another broomstick through the bottom of the skeins to serve as a weight. I let the skeins dry this way, then wind them into balls, leaving the yarn very relaxed. This method makes the yarn look as good as new.

— *Rosanna Patch, Madison, WI*

Mechanized sweater unwinding

Unravel a sweater quickly and smoothly by using a handheld electric mixer. Tie a magazine around one beater. Tape the yarn end to the magazine so it won't slip. While a helper holds the sweater, operate the mixer at low speed, unraveling the yarn and winding it at the same time.

— *Lois Abele, Springfield, VA*

Another yarn recycling tip

After unraveling the yarn from an old sweater or other knitted item you no longer wear, wind it loosely around a cake-cooling rack, then dip the rack into water and let the whole thing dry. All the kinks will be automatically smoothed out, and the yarn will be ready to wind into balls.

— *Terry Anderson, Brooksville, FL*

Straightening curly yarn

To recycle used yarn and remove the kinks, run it through this improvised steamer: Take a large coffee can and punch two holes on opposite curved sides, near the top (punch one hole from the outside and one hole from the inside). Fill the coffee can halfway with water and bring the water to a boil directly on the stove. Thread a yarn end through the holes (from the hole punched on the outside to the one punched on the inside, so the yarn doesn't snag), and place a heatproof dish over the top of the can. Mark the end with masking tape so you can find it easily, and slowly pull the yarn through, steaming the entire ball. Let the steamed yarn pile up in a basket. When the yarn has dried, wind into balls and reuse.

— *Doralee Wilson, Libby, MT*

Straightening recycled yarn

I've been reusing yarn for years. I wind it around the back of a chair and tie it in several places with little pieces of yarn. If the yarn is not new or clean, I wash it carefully. This straightens it out nicely. If the unraveled yarn is clean, I hold it over a steaming teakettle to straighten it. I keep it moving back and forth in the steam, and it straightens out almost instantly. I don't wind it into balls until I'm ready to use it.

— *Nancy B. Olson, Lake Crystal, MN*

Rejuvenating leftover yarn

Leftover or thrift-shop yarn is good for small projects such as hats or socks. But many old yarn balls are wound too tightly and need some rejuvenation. To solve this problem with wool yarns, loosely rewind the yarn into a new skein. Hang the yarn on the cardboard portion of a pants hanger in a

hot, steamy shower, then close the door or curtain tightly and leave it for several hours. The yarn will swell, and once dry, it will have new life and spring. Severely stressed yarn may have to be plumped more than once.
— *Jana Trent, Colleyville, TX*

ODDS AND ENDS
Getting the twist you want

When individual yarns or threads are being spun on a spindle or wheel, and again when two or more strands are being plied together, the wheel can be turned either clockwise or counterclockwise, resulting in a Z- or S-twist, respectively.

Clockwise twisting produces diagonal twists in the strand that slant from upper right to lower left, just like the center section of the letter Z, as shown in *Fig. 6*.

Counterclockwise twists produce diagonals that run from upper left to lower right, like the center section of the letter S. If you invert the drawing, you'll notice that the direction of the diagonals doesn't change.

The reasons for choosing one twist over another can be functional or aesthetic. To

form a multistrand yarn such as a bouclé, the spinning occurs in several steps: The individual strands may be spun in a Z-twist, then two strands plied with a Z-twist, and the third strand added with an S-twist, which binds the three strands together for stability.

Yarn untangler

If your knitting yarn becomes tangled and hard to work with, spray it with Static Guard®. Static Guard takes the kinks out of the yarn so it will knit or wind smoothly.
— *Doralee Wilson, Libby, MT*

Good use for odd skein

Try knitting your sample swatch from an odd-dye-lot skein, which yarn shops sometimes sell cheaper. I find that this helps me resist the temptation to rip out the sample and reuse the yarn. I can also tell quickly if I really want to purchase the rest of the yarn for a complete project.
— *Louise Owens, Old Hickory, TN*

Rescuing mixed-dye-lot yarns

A nonknitter friend recently bought me several skeins of yarn in a closeout sale she attended. Because she didn't know about the importance

Clockwise action

Fig. 6

Counterclockwise action

of dye lots, no two skeins were from the same lot. But I made a beautiful sweater from them by knitting and purling rows 1 and 2 from one skein and attaching a second skein for rows 3 and 4. I continued to alternate skeins every two rows. The skeins from the different dye lots made the yarns appear slightly variegated. The sweater turned out lovely, and I made good use of all the yarn.

— *Judith Nyman-Schaaf, Seattle, WA*

The skinny on pilling

Pilling happens when individual fibers slip partially out of the yarn they were spun into and are then subjected to friction, which rubs them together into those irritating little balls. It's not the presence of short fibers in a yarn that causes pilling, as many people assume. When short fibers slip out, they just fall away, but when longer fibers slip out, usually one end remains attached, so they stick around, waiting to get into trouble. The problem is related to the amount of twist in the yarn and to the amount of fiber per inch; loosely spun, thin yarns are most pill prone because these conditions make it easy for fibers to slip, and if there's a mixture of staple lengths, the problem's likely to be worse.

The longer and more uniform the staple and the more combed and tightly spun the yarn, the less pilling will occur. Good-quality worsted-spun yarns should be virtually pill free. Fiber blends can suffer from pilling because the mix may cause some of the fibers to slip more easily than others, but almost any fiber can pill. Pilling is worst where fabrics rub together, like under the arms. Machine washing and drying create lots of friction, so they will probably aggravate pilling, but a yarn that wants to pill will do so, no matter what you do. Unfortunately, I don't know of any reliable tests to predict if a yarn will pill or not.

— *Erica Lynne*

When sweaters shed

When long- and short-staple fibers are combined in a yarn, the short fibers eventually spring from the yarn and cause shedding. If shedding is pronounced, you can often turn it into an advantage. Brush the outside of the garment with a clean hairbrush to bring up a halo-like nap all over the sweater, which can be very attractive. Try it first on a small area inside the sweater to judge the effect.

— *Helen von Ammon*

TWO

HAND-KNITTING TECHNIQUES

Casting On

Left-Handed Knitting

Circular Knitting

Stitches

Ribbing

Increases and Decreases

Short Rows

Binding Off

Ripping Out and Picking Up Stitches

Odds and Ends

CASTING ON

Long-tail cast-on

The long-tail cast-on, also known as the half-hitch cast-on, is probably the most frequently used method for placing knitting stitches on the needle. It's popular because it's easy to execute and results in a neat, elastic edge.

To begin, leave a long end of yarn that's about four times the length of the edge to be cast on, and make a slip knot, as shown in *Fig. 7*. Place it on a needle in your right hand with the short end hanging on the side near you.

With the left hand, hold the short end under the last three fingers and make a loop on the left thumb. Insert the needle through the thumb loop, as shown in *Fig. 8*. With the right hand, wrap the yarn from the ball around the needle tip from left to right and lift the thumb loop over the needle tip to form a new stitch, as shown in *Fig. 9*. Repeat for the required number of stitches.

Tips for two-needle cast-on

If you cast on using the two-needle method, your cast-on edge will be firmer if you knit between the last two stitches rather than

into the last one, as seen in *Fig. 10*. Don't pull the yarn too tight, or you'll have trouble getting the needle in. With this method, you would knit the next row if you are working in stockinette stitch.

Fig. 10

Stranded cast-on

A stranded, or open-edge, cast-on results in flexible edges with easily accessed open stitches at the bottom of a piece of knitting. This is especially useful if you want to pick up and work the stitches later, or join the edge to another edge with a joinery cast-off.

To work a stranded cast-on that will be easy to remove later, begin with a main yarn and a length of contrasting yarn. Tie the main and contrasting yarns together at the end, then make a slip knot in the main yarn on a knitting needle, placing the knot on top of the needle. Hold the two strands with the contrasting yarn at the bottom, below the thumb.

Long-tail cast-on

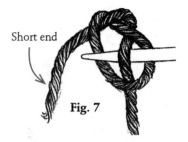

Short end

Fig. 7

Fig. 8

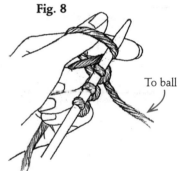

To ball

Fig. 9

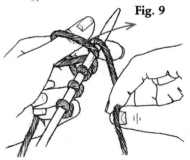

Hand-Knitting Techniques **19**

Fig. 11

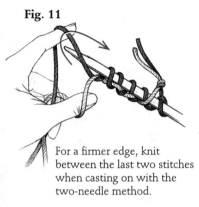

For a firmer edge, knit between the last two stitches when casting on with the two-needle method.

Fig. 12

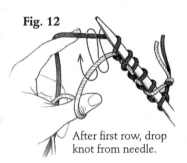

After first row, drop knot from needle.

Fig. 13

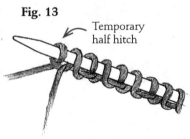

Temporary half hitch

20

Cast on by alternating two steps. For step 1, place the tip of the needle behind, then under, the forefinger strand, picking it up to form a loop on the needle *(Fig. 11)*. For step 2, place the needle tip under the thumb strand from the front, then over and behind the forefinger strand from behind, forming a second loop on the needle as shown in *Fig. 12*. Repeat these steps for the required number of stitches.

The stitches will unravel if you release the yarn ends. If you need to pause, make a temporary half hitch after a step 2 stitch by looping a strand of yarn around the needle tip, as shown in *Fig. 13*. Be sure to remove the loop before you continue.

After knitting a few rows, you'll notice that the contrasting yarn in the cast-on row simply acts as a stitch holder for the initial stitch loops, as shown in *Fig. 14*. To release the open stitches, untie the contrasting yarn and remove it.

Fig. 14

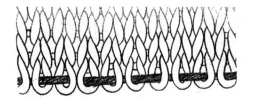

Crochet provisional cast-on

For an easy and secure invisible cast-on, you can use the crochet provisional cast-on. Use a smooth, slippery, contrasting yarn for the foundation so it will be easy to find and unravel later. Crochet a chain in the contrast yarn that is one stitch longer than the number of stitches required. Fasten off. With the knitting yarn, pick up a stitch in the back loop of each chain except the last one made, as shown in *Fig. 15*. This is the first knit row. When you're ready to pick up the loops and knit in the opposite direction, pull the contrast yarn end back through the last chain stitch and unravel the chain.

Fig. 15

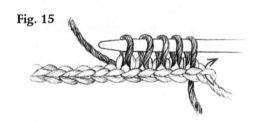

Knitting the first row

When you knit into the first row of single loop cast-on, also called single cast-on, the extra yarn between the stitches increases in length the farther you knit. To prevent this, open up each stitch as you knit it. Place the right needle into the cast-on loop and gently pull the needles apart. Then complete knitting the stitch. Keep the needles close together at this stage, and don't pull on the work. Repeating these two steps will keep the stitches open and properly spaced with no extra thread at the end.

— *Jean Lucas, Brookfield, CT*

Knit cable cast-on

For a firm edge that doesn't stretch, begin with a knit cable cast-on. You need two stitches on the needle to begin, so make one by placing a slip knot on the left needle; make the second by knitting into the first stitch and transferring the new stitch to the left needle. For subsequent stitches, insert the

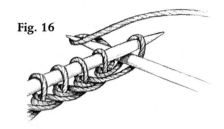

Fig. 16

right needle tip between the first two stitches on the left needle, as shown in *Fig. 16*. Draw through a loop and transfer it to the left needle. Repeat for the required number of stitches.

No stair steps when casting on

Here's a neat way to avoid knitting stair steps when casting on at the beginning or end of a row, such as you might need to do for the seams of dolman sleeves. Work to the last stitch of the row and slip it to the right needle, then turn the work. Using the cable cast-on method (shown in *Fig. 17*), insert the right needle between the first two stitches either knitwise or purlwise, as the side of the work dictates. Cast on the required number of stitches, and repeat for as many rows as you need.

— *Diane Zangl, Lomira, WI*

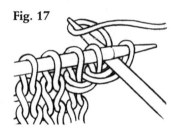

Fig. 17

At beginning of row, slip needle from front to back between first two stitches, draw through a new stitch, and place stitch on left needle. Repeat for needed stitches.

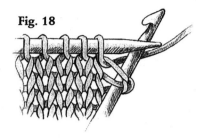

Fig. 18

Fig. 19

Fig. 20

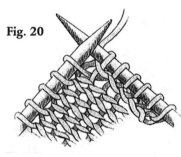

Fig. 21

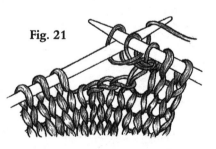

Clever cast-on at the end of a row

When you want to extend the number of stitches at the end of a row, insert a crochet hook in the edge stitch of the second row below your last stitch (see *Fig. 18*) and draw up a loop. Make a loose chain of the number of stitches to be cast on *(Fig. 19)*, then remove the hook and insert the free knitting needle into the loop to make one stitch. Pick up and knit or purl a loop in each remaining chain, bringing the needle up to the last stitch of the completed row, then continue to knit or purl across *(Fig. 20)*.

— *Janet M. Jillson, Grand Forks, ND*

Casting on midrow

To cast on stitches in the middle of a row (for example, when you're replacing the stitches you bound off for a buttonhole), use this version of the cable cast-on. Knit to the opening, then *insert the left needle between the last two stitches on the right needle. Wrap the yarn over the left needle *(Fig. 21)* and pull a stitch through. Slip this new stitch onto the right needle purlwise.* Repeat from * to * for the desired number of stitches, but slip the final stitch onto the right needle knitwise. Complete the row.

Single cast-on

When you want to make an opening in knitting, such as for buttonholes or the thumb opening in mittens, bind off or hold the required number of stitches. On the next row, use single cast-on to add back the same number of stitches above the gap. When knitting in the round, make the required number of snug loops, as shown in *Fig. 22*. The ball end of the yarn should come out behind the loop so the stitches will be firm and untwisted.

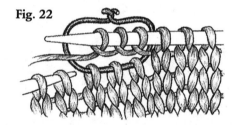

Fig. 22

LEFT-HANDED KNITTING
Southpaw basics

A left-handed person can knit just as easily as a right-handed one; you just need an understanding of the fundamentals and a little left-tailored instruction, as shown in *Figs. 23-28*.

— *Robin Ireland*

Fig. 23
Casting On

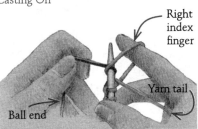

Holding the ball end of the yarn in your left hand and the yarn tail in your right, scoop a loop with the right index finger and slip it onto the needle. Carry the ball end across the needle from right to left and lift the loop over it and off the needle.

Fig. 24
Left-Handed Knit Stitch

Insert left needle from front to back of first stitch on right needle. Wrap yarn from under needle, over the top, and away; pull wrap through loop.

Fig. 25
Left-Handed Purl Stitch

Insert left needle from back to front of first stitch on right needle. Wrap yarn from over needle and pull wrap through loop.

Fig. 26
Increasing Left-Handed

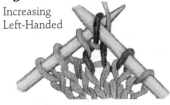

Knit into front of stitch but don't remove old loop. Insert left needle into back of loop and knit a second stitch into it.

Fig. 27
Decreasing Left-Handed

Knit Two Together (k2tog)

Insert left needle into two stitches, second stitch first, and knit them together as one stitch—decrease slants to left.

Fig. 28

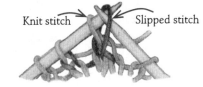

Slip, Knit, Pass Slipped Stitch Over (sl1-k1-psso)

For a right slant, slip first stitch to left needle without knitting it; knit next stitch. Using right needle, lift slipped stitch over knit stitch and off needle.

Get out your mirrors, lefties

This is the method my right-handed aunt, Emilia Mrynick, used to teach her left-handed daughter, Melanie, how to knit. Each sat on the floor facing one another, with a small mirror in her lap. By looking at Aunt Millie's hands in the mirror in Millie's lap, Melanie saw the mirror image of her mother's right-handed knitting—exactly what she should do with her own hands. And because Melanie's left-handed knitting appeared right-handed in her own mirror, Aunt Millie could easily figure out the problem whenever Melanie did something wrong.

This approach would also work for many other needle arts, like crochet, embroidery, and tatting. The only hard part is getting the mirror to stay in place, but a loop of sticky tape on its back helps hold it to your clothes. I hope this trick helps some other opposite-handed teacher-student pairs.

—*Alexandra Martin, North Plainfield, NJ*

CIRCULAR KNITTING
Tubular cast-on for circular knitting

I find it helpful, when using a tubular cast-on for circular knitting, to start as if on straight needles, with an odd number of stitches. When I've finished the tubular rows, I connect the rib into a circle by working the two end stitches together. You can work in the short tail of yarn by using it to join the gap that results when you switch from flat to circular knitting. With these few rows of work and the contrast yarn, you will be much less likely to twist the stitches in joining them.

— *Betty Klahn, Klamath Falls, OR*

Folded cast-on for double knitting

I first became aware of two-faced knitting in a French booklet, *Cahier Jardin des Model*. My problem with this tubular knitting was the cast-on selvage, which is wider than the fabric. I first tried casting on half the number of stitches and increasing on the first row. Now, however, I cast on all the stitches needed for both faces and distribute half of them onto a second double-pointed or circular needle. I fold the cast-on in half so one needle is behind the other. With the two needles in my left hand, I knit the first row onto one needle, alternating a stitch from each needle. I like to knit each face separately, knitting a stitch and slipping the next across the needle. When I turn, I knit the slipped stitches and slip the knit ones.

—*Bernice E. Barsky, New York, NY*

Getting started with knitting in the round

In case you've never tried knitting in the round on a circular needle, here are some tips to get you started: You'll need to join the cast-on row without twisting. After casting on, carefully align all stitches so they lie in the same direction. To join, hold the end of the needle with the knitting strand in your right hand, slip a marker onto this needle to indicate the beginning of the round, then knit the first stitch from the left-hand needle.

If you knit a sleeve from the cuff to the shoulder in the round, the number of cast-on stitches may be too few to fit on a circular needle. In this case, divide the stitches between three or four double-pointed needles. First, cast all stitches onto a long needle, then slip them, evenly divided, onto double-pointed needles, taking care not to twist the cast-on row. After several rows with increases have been worked, you can transfer the stitches to a short circular needle.

Circular advice

When knitting a flat article on circular needles, such as a dolman-sleeve sweater or an afghan, I use a straight needle to cast on the first row of stitches, no matter how many there are. Then, using the circular needle, I work the stitches off the straight needle according to the pattern. This assures me that my ribbing won't be twisted.

Also, to get my circular needle to behave and stay down until the weight of the garment is established, I take two or three very clean, heavyweight washers and slip them on the circular needle. They hang in the center, pulling down the nylon part of the needle. Once I've completed enough rows to pull the nylon down by itself, I slip the washers off.

— *Ann M. Prochowicz, Trempealeau, WI*

Twist-free stitches

I've discovered an easier way to start circular knitting. I use a simple half-hitch cast-on, but over two needles to match my knitting gauge. This helps keep the stitches from spiraling around the needle, making it easier to count them. So it came naturally to me to pull one needle out of half the stitches and the other needle out of the second half. I fold the work in half, with the first stitch that I cast on right next to the last and the purls in two neat rows across the bottom. There isn't the slightest risk of twist sneaking in. I begin knitting on the first stitch I cast on, which eliminates that dreadful jog at the beginning of the work; knit one-third of the stitches; pick up another needle; and knit another third. I suggest that beginners knit onto four needles in the first round, then go to three in the next round.

— *Joy Beeson, Voorheesville, NY*

Keeping the first rounds untwisted

When knitting in the round on circular needles, I use hair clips (or spring clothespins for large needles and heavier yarn) to keep the newly cast-on stitches and first few rounds from twisting. Snap one on over the stitches and needle every 15 to 20 stitches. They will slide onto the cable easily and need only a little care when coming back onto the left needle. When the knitting is established, you can take them off.

— *Louise Owens, Old Hickory, TN*

Even joins in circular knitting

Here are two techniques for making perfectly smooth rounds of circular knitting with no perceptible joins:

On the cast-on edge, turn and knit back the first row (as for straight knitting), and then join, making certain the edges aren't twisted. This will eliminate the "dog leg," or uneven join, and reverse the cast-on edge to the more attractive, unstranded side (with the garter-stitch bumps). Be sure to establish ribbing or other pattern in straight knit in the first row, and then join for circular knitting.

When you cast off in the round, you can eliminate the uneven join by inserting the needle into the first bound-off stitch, making a stitch, then binding it off as the final

bound-off stitch. This technique pulls the first portion up to make it even with the last stitch, but the double stitch is not noticeable.
— *Barbara Rottman, Urbana, OH*

Avoiding the dog leg in circular knitting

My solution is to cast on by using a double technique with one needle and two ends of yarn. At the join, I pick up the "tail" and, holding it together with the working yarn, I draw the last and first cast-on stitches closely together. I work the first four stitches with both yarns, then drop the tail and work on. Since there's no knot with a double cast-on, the stitches will slide together, and you'll have to use a marker to find the beginning of the round.
— *Shelagh Smith, Brandon, VT*

Textured knitting on circular needles

When I began searching for textured-knit directions written for circular needles, I discovered that there are precious few. However, with a little ingenuity, you can convert directions for straight-needle patterns to circular-knitting directions.

First, determine if the odd- or even-numbered rows are on the right side of the piece. Make a swatch on straight needles. This will also help when you start your conversions, since you'll be able to relate the actual knitting to the printed instructions.

Write down every step in this process, and begin by copying the original directions, one row per line and only one repeat of the pattern. Be sure to write down the "end whatever" part of the directions, as you would if you were knitting only one repeat of the pattern. Although the logical place to note the beginning and end of a pattern repeat might seem to be between the asterisks, they aren't always placed at the same point from one row to the next in the pattern, so don't jump to conclusions about how the pattern works yet.

Next, recopy the right-side rows from left to right, just as they appear in the original instructions. But write down the wrong-side rows from right to left, copying in the reverse order. Begin with the "end whatever" stitches. Then draw arrows from each stitch on a lower row to the stitch in the row above into which it gets worked, and circle

Stitch Equivalents When Converting from Straight-Needle to Circular Knitting

Wrong-side stitches	Right-side equivalents
P (purl)	K (knit)
K (knit)	P (purl)
P-b (purl in back)	K-b (knit in back)
K-b (knit in back)	P-b (purl in back)

Increases	
P into back and front	K into front and back
P into front and back	K into back and front
K into back and front	P into front and back
K into front and back	P into back and front

Decreases	
P2tog	K2tog
P2tog-b	Sl 1, k1, psso (slip, knit, pass slipped st over), or work ssk (slip, slip, knit 2 slipped sts together).
K2tog	P2tog
K2tog-b	P2tog-b
Sl 1, k1, psso	P2tog-b
P3tog	K3tog
K3tog	P3tog

the "end whatever" stitches. These are the same as the "plus y" stitches added to any pattern multiple (which usually reads as "multiple of x plus y"). Rewriting the wrong-side rows and drawing the arrows may seem like a lot of extra work, but it cuts down immensely on the confusion that might arise when you're making the conversions. The only time I don't make this diagram is when all of the wrong-side rows are knit or purl stitches in very obvious places, such as purling the wrong side on a cable stitch.

Stitch Equivalents When Converting from Straight-Needle to Circular Knitting (cont.)

P2tog pnso (pass next st over). *Work:* P2tog, sl next st to RH needle kwise, replace on LH needle in new orientation, replace p2tog on LH needle, pass sl st on LH needle over p2tog, transfer p2tog back to RH needle.	Sl1, k2tog, psso
Sl k2tog psso	P2tog pnso

Twist stitches

Cross L, knit (skip 1st st, k 2nd st in back, k skipped st in front, slip both sts tog to RH needle). *Alternative method:* Skip 1st st and k 2nd st, slip both sts tog to RH needle.	Cross L, purled.
Cross L, purled	
Cross R, knit (skip 1st st, k 2nd st in front, k skipped st in front, slip both sts tog to RH needle). *Alternative method:* K2tog, leaving sts on LH needle; insert RH needle from front between 2 sts and k 1st st again; sl both sts tog from needle.	Cross R, purled.
Cross R, purled.	Cross R, knit.

After you know which is the right side of your pattern and which stitches get worked into which other stitches, you're ready to begin the conversion process. If you're planning to use the pattern completely around the garment, you must change "multiple of x plus y stitches" to "multiple of x plus nothing" The "plus y" stitches are for a border on each side of the pattern, so when you knit in the round, you don't want them. When preparing your diagram, make sure that you mark the "plus y" or "end" stitches so they'll be easy to eliminate later. If you're planning to use the pattern as a vertical section on the garment, you'll probably want to include the border areas to set one pattern off from another.

As you write out the new directions, the right-side rows remain the same, minus the "plus y" stitches, if you've decided to omit them. You can begin your directions at any point within the pattern, but if you start with a solid area, you'll avoid awkward, lacy stitches at your change-of-round point. Just don't omit any of the pattern stitches. Refer to the stitch equivalent chart to get the right-side equivalent for each wrong-side stitch. Simply substitute the equivalents in the same order that you've written the wrong-side directions.

When you've completed your conversions, you'll need to work a gauge swatch. Knitting done in the round, only on the right side, results in a slightly different gauge than knitting worked back and forth on both sides. You can use double-pointed needles to make a small cylindrical swatch. Three repeats of the pattern often work well, since you'll have completed patterns on each

needle. The disadvantage of a cylindrical swatch is that it may be difficult to measure accurately unless you put more repeats on each needle.

Making a flat swatch on circular needles is quicker and more reliable when I use this method: Cast on a sufficient number of stitches, and knit one row to give yourself a firm base. Include the "plus y" border stitches for an edge on this flat swatch, even if you won't be using them in your garment. Then work the first "round" of your new pattern directions. At the end of the round, cut the yarn and slide the work around to the other end of the needle to start the next "round." Each round begins with the same stitch, and you always have the right side of the knit fabric facing you. To reduce the number of cut threads, pull out enough yarn to work the second round and other even-numbered rounds from the middle of the strand toward the tail. Then, when you push the swatch around to the other side of the needle, work the third round and other odd-numbered rounds from the middle of the strand (where you began the previous round) toward the ball. Cut the yarn at the end of each odd-numbered round. This leaves all loose ends on the same edge of the work. If necessary, adjust your gauge by changing the needle size so unbroken patterns go around your garment's circumference.

— *Marilyn Moss*

Straight to circular conversions

Marilyn Moss makes heavy weather out of a relatively easy revision from straight to circular needles. A swatch is always necessary, both for gauge and to determine how the pattern develops. Once you know which is the right side (odd or even), you work right-side rows as usual from left to right and alternate rows from end to beginning, substituting knit for purl and vice versa. If the pattern is very complex, you're better off reading Barbara Walker's instructions for charting the pattern and working it out on 5-square-per-inch graph paper, especially if you're combining lace or cable patterns.

— *Etta deVee Suggs, San Francisco, CA*

STITCHES
Slipping a stitch

Slipping one stitch purlwise (sl 1 pwise) is a way to move a stitch to the right needle without knitting it. Slipping the stitch purlwise also ensures that it will not be twisted when you encounter it on the next row. On right-side rows, with the yarn in back, insert the right needle as if to purl, slipping the stitch in this position onto the needle (see *Fig. 29*). On wrong-side rows, do the same, except with the yarn in front.

On slipping stitches

Many knitters automatically slip a stitch as if to knit the stitch—this seems the most natural motion. But unless the pattern specifies to slip the stitch knitwise, it should always be slipped purlwise: The right needle should be inserted into the next stitch through the right side of the stitch. This allows the slipped stitch to lie in the same direction on the needle as the other stitches. In this manner, the slipped stitch will work off flat in the next row, with no twists to cause irregularities in your fabric.

— *Hannah James*

Fig. 29

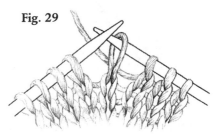

Knit wrapping yarn twice.

Fig. 30

Yarn over between two knit stitches

Yarn over

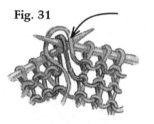

Bring yarn between needles to front, then over right needle to back.

Fig. 31

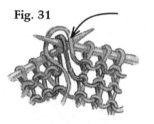

Yarn over between two purl stitches.

Take yarn over right needle to back, then between needles to front.

Fig. 32

Yarn over

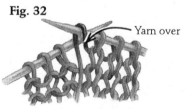

Yarn over after a purl stitch and before a knit stitch.

Take yarn over right needle to back.

Yarn over ins and outs

The yarn over stitch is worked differently depending on whether a knit or purl stitch precedes and follows it. However, many instructions give only the abbreviation yo or just o, so knowing which way to wrap the yarn can be difficult. European instructions often use wf (wool forward), which simply means to bring the yarn to the front of the work.

Generally, the yarn over should lie in the same direction as the other stitches on the needle, with the stitch slanting down to the right in front of the needle. The stitch is completed in the following row, when it is knit, purled, or slipped, just like any other stitch.

Yarn over between two knit stitches: When the stitches before and after the yarn over are knit stitches, just bring the yarn from the back of the work (where you held it for knitting) to the front between the needle points. Then take it back over the top of the right needle and continue knitting, as shown in *Fig. 30*. For the next stitch, you'll be knitting with the yarn held as if to purl.

In the following row, work the yarn over as a regular stitch *(Fig. 33)*, whether it is a

knit, purl, or slip stitch—this will create the hole. The abbreviations for this yarn over include yo (yarn over), yf (yarn forward), wf (wool forward), yfon (yarn forward and over needle), and wfon (wool forward and over needle).

Yarn over after a knit stitch and before a purl stitch: Bring the yarn from the back to the front between the needle points. Wrap it around the right needle and again bring it between the needles to the front *(Fig. 35)*. Purl the next stitch. The abbreviations are yfrn and wfrn (yarn or wool forward and around needle).

Yarn over between two purl stitches: Take the yarn from the front over the right needle to the back, then bring it between the needle points to the front again, as shown in *Fig. 31*. The abbreviations are yrn and wrn (yarn or wool around needle).

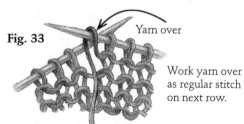

Fig. 33

Yarn over

Work yarn over as regular stitch on next row.

Yarn over after a purl stitch and before a knit stitch: Take the yarn from the front over the right needle to the back *(Fig. 32)*. Knit the next stitch. The yarn is not brought between the needle points, as in the previous three methods. The abbreviations are yon and won (yarn or wool over needle).

Yarn over before working a first stitch: When the first stitch in a row is a yarn over, the techniques are slightly different. For a yarn over before a knit stitch, put the right needle under the yarn and begin to knit *(Fig. 34)*. For a yarn over before a purl stitch, put the right needle under the yarn, bring the yarn from the back to the font between the needle points *(Fig. 36)*, and purl.

Decreasing with yarn overs: If a yarn over is not to be an increase, it must be accompanied by a decrease, in the same row or in one of the following two or three rows so that the established number of stitches is maintained. Several decreases can accompany yarn overs; the method used will alter the appearance of the work. One of the most common is k2tog (knit two together), which is a right-slanting decrease. If your pattern calls for just one type of decrease, it is usually k2tog. Ssk (slip, slip, knit), sl 1, k1, psso (slip one, knit one, pass slipped stitch over), and k2tog tbl (knit two together through back loops) are all left-slanting decreases. Ssk means to slip two stitches one at a time knitwise onto the right needle, then to insert

Fig. 34

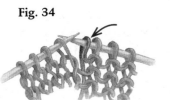

Yarn over before first knit stitch.

Put needle under yarn and begin to knit.

Fig. 35

Yarn over after a knit stitch and before a purl stitch.

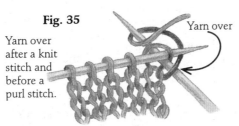

Bring yarn between needles to front, around right needle to back, and between needles again to front.

Fig. 36

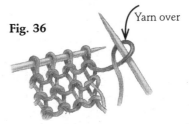

Yarn over before first purl stitch.

Put right needle under yarn, take yarn over right needle to back, then bring between needles to front.

the tip of the left needle into the fronts of the two stitches and knit them together. This is the neatest of the left-slanting decreases and the one that most nearly matches the right-slanting k2tog decrease for a symmetrical decrease on either side of a central stitch. It can be used any time sl 1, k1, psso is called for.

When executing a yarn over followed by a sl 1, k1, psso decrease, make sure you pass the slipped stitch, not the yarn over, over the knit stitch. Slipping the yarn over is an easy error to make.

Elongated stitch: Another form of yarn over used in pattern stitches is an elongated stitch. This stitch is made when the yarn is wrapped two or more times around the needle. The yarn overs are dropped in the following row to create a long stitch. The instructions for this stitch are y2on, y4on, (wrap yarn two times, or four times, around needle), or 00, 000 (wrap the yarn once for each 0). The instruction to drop the yarn overs is drop yo or drop wf. For an elongated stitch, the yarn should be wrapped as for a regular yarn over, based on the stitches that precede and follow it.

— *Shirley W. MacNulty*

34

Elongated stitches

Wrapping yarn around the needle twice is a way to make one stitch twice as tall as the others. Insert the right needle into a stitch as if to knit, then bring the yarn over the top of the needle to the back, under the needle to the front, then over the top again before knitting the stitch *(Fig. 37)*. On the return row, drop one of the loops and work the other as directed, knitting, purling, or slipping it.

Another useful technique to produce elongated stitches is to knit into the row below. Insert the right needle knitwise into the stitch below the one on the left needle *(Fig. 38)*. Knit and drop the top stitch, which will be caught in the stitch you've just knit.

This bc4 (back cross cable over four stitches) looks different from a standard back cross cable because it is worked with elongated slipped stitches. In a back cross cable, you move stitches from the left to the right on the front of the work. Slip two stitches purlwise to a cable needle and hold them behind the work; knit the next two stitches; then knit the two stitches from the cable needle, wrapping the yarn twice for each stitch (*Fig. 39*). The effect is that you have traded position between two purl stitches and two elongated knit stitches. The purls become elongated knits, and the elongated knits will become purls on the next row.

This fc4 (front cross cable over four stitches) looks different from a standard front cross cable because it is worked with elongated slipped stitches. The process is the same as bc4 except that you're moving stitches toward the left by holding them in front of the work, and the elongated stitches are not knit from the cable needle. In a front cross cable, you move stitches from the right to the left on the front of the work. Slip the next two stitches purlwise to the cable needle and hold them in front of the work; knit the next two stitches, wrapping the yarn twice for each stitch; then knit the two stitches from the cable needle (*Fig. 40*).

Tool-less twists

For twist stitches, you don't need a cable needle, cable hook, or any other tool. For a left twist, slip the two stitches one at a time as if to knit, then put the needle through both and slip them back, as shown in the top

Fig. 37
Knit the wrapping yarn twice.

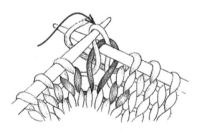

Fig. 38
Knit into row below.

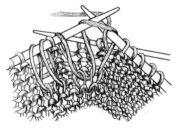

Fig. 39
Back cross cable over four stitches.

Fig. 40
Front cross cable over four stitches.

Fig. 41

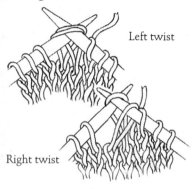

Left twist

Right twist

drawing of *Fig. 41*. To make a right twist, slip both stitches as if to knit two together, then slip them back one at a time, as shown in the bottom drawing of *Fig. 41*. All slips should be made knitwise so that the twists untwist and you end up with the stitches front side to the front.

— *Joy Beeson, Voorheesville, NY*

Cast-on bobble

Using a cable cast-on to add stitches at any point in a garment between the first two stitches on the left needle is good for making a cast-on bobble. Insert the right needle tip between the next two stitches on the left needle, as shown in *Fig. 42.* Draw through a loop and transfer it to the left needle. Repeat for the required number of stitches.

Fig. 42

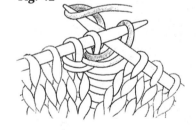

Easy bobbles

I crochet, rather than knit, bobbles in my sweaters. I yarn over onto the hook to start and make five double crochets in the bobble stitch, holding back one loop of each on the hook. I pull the yarn through all the loops on the hook, then replace the stitch on the knitting needle, pushing the bobble through to the correct side. I find the results identical to knitted bobbles, and the work need not be turned.

— *Catherine Ham, Austin, TX*

Wisp knitting

Knitters can produce the same plush, textured rugs, wall hangings, and pillows that are produced by latch hookers. This simple technique is for those who prefer working with a pliable yarn backing rather than a rigid canvas; who like to use up their yarn scraps; who enjoy watching their work grow, rather than "counting down" rows on a canvas; and who are happy to move on to another project when the first is complete, without binding, sizing, and finishing.

The wisps are cut lengths of yarn that are tied onto the yarn before it is knit. The wisps may be any length, and depending on the yarn weight, they may be single or double strands (attached separately). Before buying materials, make a sample to learn the technique and determine if the wisps should be single or double. The basic stitch is worked in worsted yarn for wall hangings and pillows, and in heavier yarn to provide body and strength for rugs.

To make the sample, use worsted yarn and size 8 needles. To master the stitch, work the first section without attaching wisps. Cast on 15 stitches.

Row 1:
Purl across row.

Row 2:
K1; *bring yarn forward, sl 1, bring yarn back; k1. Repeat from * across row.

Row 3:
Purl across row.

Row 4:
With yarn forward, sl 1, bring yarn back; *k1; bring yarn forward, sl 1, bring yarn back, repeat from * across row.

Continue until 9 rows are completed. Look at your work to determine the pattern of the slipped stitches.

Row 10:
Now you'll begin tying wisps onto the base yarn at the beginning of each row. Tie on 7 wisps (in general, tie on enough to work a whole row) as follows: Double the wisp strand and bring the two cut ends around the base yarn and through the looped end. Pull

on the two ends to form a half-hitch knot. Follow the instructions for Row 2, slip a wisp into place after each yarn forward, slip the next stitch, and lock the wisp into place with a yarn back; then k1.

Continue in the pattern. Use 8 wisps on the next knit row and alternate between 7 and 8 until the sample is square. Bind off on a purl row.

The needle, yarn size, and tension help determine the proper wisp spacing. To determine spacing, work a row with wisps. Then rip it and measure the distance between them. Use this to guide your spacing when tying on wisps.

Once you master the wisp-stitch technique, you can use it for any knit item. You must make allowances for the gauge of the base stitch when you are "grafting" wisps to a knit pattern, but usually the wisp stitch can be used for many practical, decorative items without pattern changes.

— *Margaret S. Peterson, Marshfield, WI*

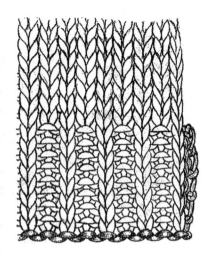

Fig. 43

RIBBING
Double-layer rib

A double-layer rib gives firmness and body to ribbed edges, which can be more compatible with the weight of a heavy garment than a single-layer rib. In ribbing, knit the width of the band normally. To create a fold line, purl a right-side row or knit a wrong-side row, then resume the ribbing stitch and knit the same number of rows again for the second layer, as shown in *Fig. 43*. With this technique, you can sandwich the raw edge of a garment's lining between the layers of ribbing, then sew the ribbing and lining in place with one row of overcast stitching.

Perfect ribbing from the neck down

To prevent a loose or bunchy ribbing when working in a standard pattern such as knit one, purl one or knit two, purl two, decrease the total number of stitches by 10 percent just before starting the ribbing pattern. Space the decreases evenly around the sweater by working every ninth and tenth stitch together as one. Also, don't bind off the ribbing too tightly, or the bound-off edge will become rigid. If necessary, when working the bind-off row, use a needle four or five sizes larger than the one you used for the rib.

Sometimes the knit stitches in ribbing open up and look rather loose. To prevent this, knit into the back loops of the knit stitches on every right-side row (on every other round in circular knitting).
— *Barbara Walker*

Elastic knit ribbing for cotton

Here's a method for achieving elastic ribbing in inelastic yarns such as cotton. You slip the purl stitches with the yarn in front and work only the knit stitches in the first and last two rows. The slipped rows have less yarn and keep the ribbing from stretching. This method is for an even number of stitches in a knit one, purl one rib. It doesn't work for knit two, purl two rib. Cast on as directed.

Row 1:
K1, sl 1 wyif, bring yarn to back.
Repeat across row.

Row 2:
Repeat Row 1.

Row 3:
K1, p1 across row as usual.

Repeat Row 3 until ribbing is two rows less than desired length. Then repeat Row 1 twice. Any increase must be done in the first row of the body, rather than in the last row of the ribbing, which is what you would normally do anyway.
— *Flo Patton, Andrews, TX*

No-purl corrugated rib

Purling the multicolor stripes of Fair Isle corrugated rib gives an unappealing echo of the previous color in the new one. Changing the colors on the knit stripes solves that problem, but since you're stranding two yarns, the rib isn't stretchy like normal knit two, purl two rib.

I take advantage of this "drawback." First, I knit all the stitches (no purling), so the color always changes cleanly. Then, I pull the stranded yarn tight in back so the rib puckers like corrugated paper. I'm careful to calculate enough stitches to go over the head and hands and around the hips. I alternate knitting two stitches in a main color and shading the next two stitches over the length of the rib from darkest to lightest and back to darkest with yarn from a contrasting color family. To prevent the edge from curling, I pick up the cast-on and add a knit facing later, stitching it inside loosely.
— *Alice DeCamp, Westport, CT*

Stretchy knit ribbing

Here's a delicate ribbing called plissé that is very stretchy and yet hugs the waistline beautifully. Use the same needle size as you would to knit any ribbing, and cast on your stitches in multiples of three. Work each row knit two, purl one as deep as desired *(Fig. 44)*.
— *Clara Wendrich, Tampa, FL*

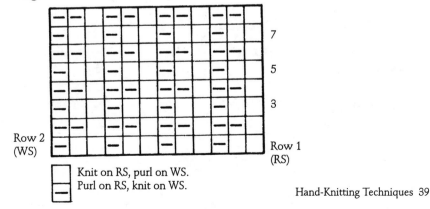

Fig. 44 Chart shows right side of fabric.

Row 2 (WS)

Row 1 (RS)

7

5

3

☐ Knit on RS, purl on WS.
▬ Purl on RS, knit on WS.

INCREASES AND DECREASES
Paired increases and decreases

Decreases and increases in knits can slant either to the left or to the right, adding decorative detail to the knitted fabric. When knitting pairs of increases for a dart, for example, you might balance the dart by working one right-slanting and one left-slanting increase together, or you could slant all the increases toward the outside of the garment. There are many different increases and decreases to choose from, including the following, shown in *Fig. 45*.

Right-slanting decrease: Knit two together (k2tog) by inserting the right needle into the next two stitches on the left needle and knitting as one.

Left-slanting decrease: Called slip, slip, knit (ssk), this decrease is worked by first slipping two stitches knitwise, one at a time, to the right needle; insert the left needle tip from left to right into the front of the slipped stitches, then knit them off together.

Right-slanting increase: Lift the purl loop below the next stitch and place it on the left needle; knit the loop as a normal stitch, then knit the next stitch.

Left-slanting increase: This increase is worked like the right-slanting increase, but *after* the stitch: Knit the stitch, then lift the purl loop two rows below the stitch; untwist the loop, then knit it as a normal stitch.

Fig. 45

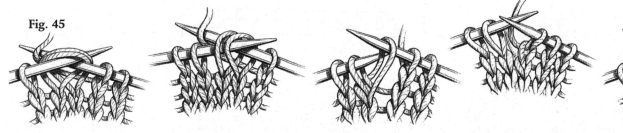

Right-slanting decrease   Left-slanting decrease   Right-slanting increase   Left-slanting increase   3-in-1 decrease

3-in-1 decrease: Knit three together by inserting the right needle into all three stitches on the left needle and knitting as one.

3-in-1 increase: Work a right-slanting increase, knit the stitch, then work a left-slanting increase on the other side.

Paired increases and decreases for raglan sweaters

It is essential to use paired increases when you knit the shoulder area of a raglan from the top down and paired decreases for the sleeves from armhole to wrist. The complementary slants produced will give a garment an elegant, professional look.

Paired increases: Although I worked all these increases with a single-stitch seamline, you can work some with multiple seam stitches in ribbing or cable pattern. All the pairs shown are repeated every other row. Work one method at each of four seamlines for the eight increases of a raglan sweater.

1. **Bar increase:** Single or multiple seam stitches. Produces a small bar across the stockinette side. Increase (knit in front, knit in back) in the stitch before the seamline, and increase (knit in front, knit in back) in the only (or last) seamline stitch.

2. **Double increase in single stitch (open):** Knit, yarn over, knit in single seam stitch.

3. **Double increase in single stitch (closed):** Knit seam stitch, knit in seam stitch in row below, knit seam stitch.

4. **Double increase in single stitch (invisible):** Knit in seam stitch in row below, knit seam stitch, knit in seam stitch two rows below.

5. **Yarn over increase:** Single or multiple seam stitches. Yarn over, knit seam stitch(es), yarn over.

6. **Raised method (visible):** Single or multiple seam stitches. Work to first seam stitch. With left needle, pick up running thread between needles from front and knit from front. Knit seam stitch(es). With left needle, pick up running thread between needles after last seam stitch from front and knit from front.

7. Raised method (invisible): Single or multiple seam stitches. Work to seam stitch. With left needle, pick up running thread between needles from back, and knit from front (right-hand slant crossed stitch). Knit seam stitch(es). With left needle, pick up running thread between needles after last seam stitch from front, and knit from back (left-hand crossed stitch).

8. Lifted method (invisible): Single or multiple seam stitches. Work to stitch before seam stitch. Knit in stitch below first stitch on left needle. Knit stitch before seam stitch. Knit seam stitch(es). Knit stitch after seam stitch. Knit in stitch two rows below stitch on right needle.

Paired decreases: Put a left-side decrease near the beginning of the row and a right-side decrease near the end of the same row. In raglans knit from the bottom up, make paired decreases as instructed below.

1. Popular decrease: RH/LH slants: These smooth decrease lines are used for full-fashioning and vertical darts.

Right of seamline:
Work to two stitches before seamline, k2tog, knit seam stitch(es).

Left of seamline:
Ssk (slip two stitches knitwise, knit together).

2. Accented decrease: LH/RH slants:

Right of seamline:
Work to two stitches before seamline, ssk, knit seam stitch(es).

Left of seamline:
K2tog.

3. Easy-match decrease: RH/LH slants. This technique is better if your k2tog and ssk decreases aren't a good match.

Right of seamline:
Work to two stitches before seamline, insert right needle into second stitch on left needle as if to purl and lift it over the first stitch, knit one, knit seam stitch(es).

Left of seamline:
Slip two stitches to right needle as if to knit, pass first slipped stitch over second, transfer remaining stitch to left needle, knit one.

4. Feather decrease: Double LH/double RH slants: This technique adds attractive detail and texture. Repeat every fourth row for a 45° angle. You may do triple decreases in the same way, repeating them every sixth row for the same angle.

Right of seamline:
Work to four stitches before seamline. Slip first two stitches as if to knit onto a cable needle and hold in front. *Knit first stitch on cable needle and first stitch on left needle together. Repeat from *.

Left of seamline:
Slip two stitches as if to knit onto cable needle and hold in back. *Knit first stitch on left needle and first stitch on cable needle together. Repeat from *.

 5. Yarn over decreases: RH/LH slants (decrease two, add one): This style adds a decorative touch to smooth fabric or blends well with yarn over and fagoted patterns.

Right of seamline:
Work to three stitches before seamline. K3tog, yarn over.

Left of seamline:
Yarn over, slip one, ssk, psso.
 — *B. Borssuck*

Make one

To make one stitch (a type of increase) on the purl or knit side, lift the running thread between the stitches on the right and left needles onto the point of the left needle by inserting the left needle from front to back. Knit or purl the new stitch in the back as shown in *Fig. 46;* it will be twisted. Working the make one stitch twisted prevents a hole from forming below it.

Two common decreases

There are several ways to decrease stitches in knitting, and among the most common are slip, slip, knit (ssk) and purl two together (p2tog). Worked on the knit side of the fabric, the ssk decrease slants to the left: Slip two stitches, one at a time, as if to knit. Insert the left needle into these stitches from left to right, as shown in *Fig. 47,* and knit them together.

Fig. 46

Make one increase

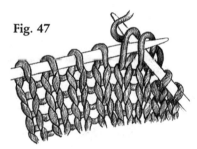

Fig. 47

Slip, slip, knit decrease (ssk)

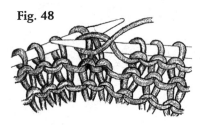

Fig. 48

Purl two together decrease (p2tog)

Fig. 49

Knit two together decrease (k2tog)

Worked on the purl side of the fabric, the p2tog decrease slants to the right on the knit face of the fabric. To p2tog, insert the right needle into two adjacent stitches and purl them together (*Fig. 48*).

Knit two together decrease

The usual way to decrease in knitting is to k2tog (knit two stitches together). This decrease slants toward the right. Insert the right needle knitwise through two stitches at once as shown in *Fig. 49* and knit them together as if they were one stitch.

Purl two together–back

A p2tog-b decrease (purl two stitches together through the back loops) is the purl-side equivalent of a slip, slip, knit (ssk) decrease. This decrease slants toward the left on the purl side. Turn the work over slightly and insert the tip of the right needle into the backs of the next two purl stitches on the left needle, second stitch first; then wrap the yarn and purl them as one stitch (*Fig. 50*).

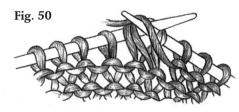

Fig. 50

Purl two together–back decrease (p2tog-b)

Improving the ssk

A favorite knitting technique of mine for decreases that slant to the left is the ssk (slip, slip, knit), but instead of slipping the two stitches as if to knit, I slip the first stitch as if to knit and the second as if to purl. Then I insert the left needle to the front of both slipped stitches and knit them together as usual. The slipped purlwise stitch somehow tucks itself very neatly behind the slipped knitwise stitch and becomes invisible, resulting in a very smooth decrease that slants to the left. Use this method whenever the directions say sl 1, k1, psso, and you'll get a much neater edge.

—*E. Dee Barrington, Ponca City, OK*

Left-slanting decrease

Sl 1, k1, psso (slip one, knit one, pass slipped stitch over) is a single decrease that slants toward the left. Slip the first stitch as if to knit. Knit the next stitch. Insert the tip of the left needle into the slipped stitch, as shown in *Fig. 51,* and pull it over the knitted stitch.

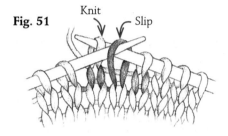

Fig. 51   Knit   Slip

Vertical double decrease

Sl2tog kwise, k1, p2sso (slip two together knitwise, knit one, pass two slipped stitches over) is a vertical double decrease. The two side stitches slant inward behind the prominent center stitch. Slip two stitches as if knitting them together, knit the next stitch, and pass the two slipped stitches together over the knit stitch, as shown in *Fig. 52.*

Lifted increase

The lifted increase adds a stitch almost invisibly. When you get to the point of the increase, insert the right needle into the top of the next stitch in the row below; knit as shown in *Fig. 53.* Knit the next stitch on the left needle.

Perfectly matched decreases

As every knitter knows, when you're working a series of decreases every other row, none of the left-slanting decreases (sl 1, k1, psso; k2tog through back loop; or ssk) will produce a truly straight decrease line exactly matching the line of the right-slanting k2tog ones. Now try this: For your right-slanting decreases, k2tog every other knit row as usual, but for your left-slanting decreases, work slip, slip, purl (ssp) on the purl side. To ssp, slip the first two stitches one at a time knitwise (just as you would

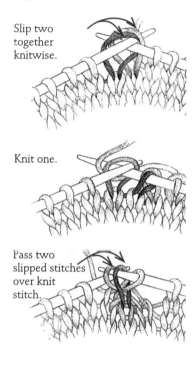

Fig. 52

Slip two together knitwise.

Knit one.

Pass two slipped stitches over knit stitch.

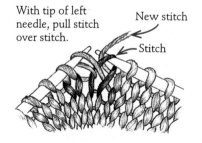

Fig. 53

With tip of left needle, pull stitch over stitch.

New stitch

Stitch

Fig. 54

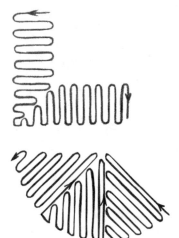

Knit a border with mitered corners using short rows or make a circle with short-row wedges.

with ssk)—this twists each stitch. Now replace both stitches, still twisted, onto the left needle and purl them together through the back loops. You'll find that your decrease lines will match perfectly, and both will look as straight as if they had been drawn with a ruler.

—*Janet E. Price, Chicago, IL*

SHORT ROWS
Short rows: The secret is wrapping

A short row is a row (or round in circular knitting) that's not worked all the way from one end to the other. You may stop at any point on the row, turn, and work in the opposite direction. Short rows are handy for shaping:

- Shape the shoulders or raise the back of the neck of a sweater with short rows; you'll eliminate the need for "stair-step" bits of binding-off.

- Incorporate short rows across the back of the tubular body of a seamless sweater to prevent riding up.
- Use short rows to form neat, mitered corners on a border worked around a square blanket, or knit a series of pie wedges with graduating short rows to form the circle of a round throw or tam-o'-shanter *(Fig. 54).*
- Shape bust darts, elbow darts, high-fashion knit drapes, ruffles, gathers, and assorted protuberances.

Short rows are best worked in stockinette stitch, ribbing, or garter stitch. But, if you just turn in the middle of a round or row and work back, you'll get a huge hole where you turned. If you slip the first stitch after the turn, you'll get a smaller but still visible hole. Here's where wrapping comes in. Barbara Walker truly tamed the technique in *Knitting from the Top;* the technique got its name from David Xenakis.

When you get to the turning place, leave the working yarn where it is—in back if you're knitting, in front if you're purling. Slip the next stitch onto the right needle and carry the working yarn to the other side of the knitting, as shown in *Fig. 55.* Replace the slipped stitch onto the left needle, turn, and you're ready to work the short row. The working yarn has been wrapped around the base of the unworked stitch, as shown in *Fig. 56.* You perform this process exactly the same way for knit or purl, but always keep the wrap fairly loose.

When you meet a wrap on the knit side that you made on the knit side, you can dig the right needle into the wrap and the stitch and knit them together, as shown in *Fig. 57,* or place the slipped stitch onto the right needle, pick up the wrap on the left needle, replace the slipped stitch, and knit the two together.

When you meet a wrap on the knit side that you made on the purl side, there are three things you can do: (1) Knit the stitch and wrap together as shown in *Fig. 57,* (2) slip the wrap, knit the stitch, and pass the slipped wrap over (psso), or (3) slip the wrap, slip the stitch, insert the tip of the left

Fig. 55

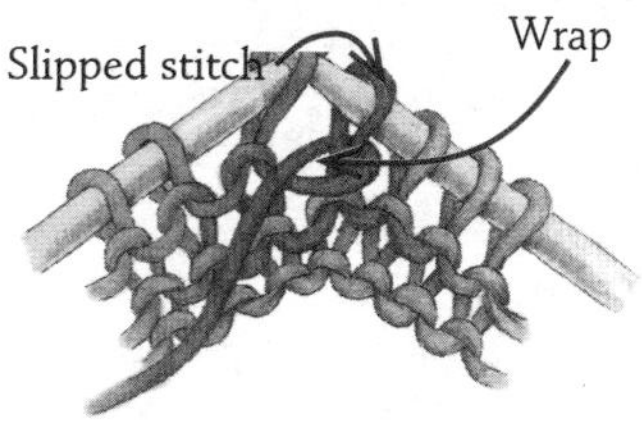

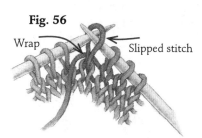

Carry working yarn to opposite side before replacing slipped stitch on left needle.

Fig. 56

Wrapping prevents a large space from developing between worked and unworked stitches.

Fig. 57

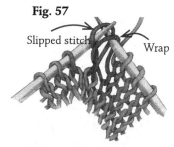

On knit side, work wrap made on knit side by knitting wrap and slipped stitch together.

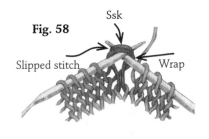

Fig. 58

Ssk

Slipped stitch   Wrap

For a knit-side wrap made on
the purl side, slip the wrap, slip a
stitch, then insert left needle and
knit them together (ssk).

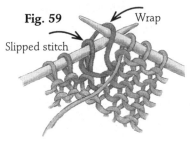

Fig. 59   Wrap

Slipped stitch

For a purled wrap on a purl side,
lift back of wrap and place on
left needle.

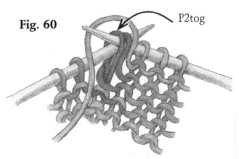

Fig. 60   P2tog

Then slip right needle into wrap
and slipped stitch and purl
both together.

needle into these two stitches, and knit them
together (ssk), as shown in *Fig. 58.*

When you meet a wrap on the purl side
that you made on the purl side, lift the back
of the wrap (which is actually on the knit
side of the work) and put it on the left needle
(Fig. 59). Then purl the two together *(Fig. 60).*

Short rows in garter stitch are even easier
to make. It is impossible to make the wraps
invisible, since two ridges will suddenly
become one, but it will be least noticeable if
you perform the wrap. The spot where the
wrap strangles the slipped stitch makes a
little horizontal bump that looks like a purl.

— *Meg Swansen*

Short-row basics

Knitting short rows is a nearly invisible
method of shaping a knitted piece. A short
row is any portion of the row less than a full
row. Whether knitting by hand or machine,
short rows are always worked in pairs. To
work short rows by hand, you simply stop
partway in a row, turn the work, and purl
back over that section, then turn again and
continue knitting, as shown in *Fig. 61.* By

Fig. 61

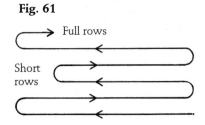

Full rows

Short
rows

machine, the process is the same: Select the needles you want to knit using the hold position or pushers, knit a partial row, then knit back on the same stitches, and continue knitting.

If you place extra rows in the middle of a section of knitting, making each short row a little longer than the previous one until you're knitting full rows, you'll cause the fabric to bulge outward or curve downward. Short rows can be used to construct seamless darts, sock heels, mitered corners, spheres, ruffles, or gathers.

The only problem with knitting short rows is that holes can form at the turn. There are two ways to prevent these holes. The first is to decrease the total stitch count at the turn by knitting or purling two stitches together.

The second method, which maintains the stitch count, is to wrap the yarn around the stitch after the turn. *Fig. 62* shows how to wrap the yarn when knitting by hand. Work to the turn, slip the next stitch from the left to right needle as if to purl, bring the yarn to the front (for knitting) or back (for purling), then slip the stitch back to the left needle. Return the yarn to the other side, turn, and work the short row, starting at the first stitch

on the left needle. When you are ready to work the wrapped stitch, scoop the wrap up with the stitch, reposition the left needle, and work the two together.

If you're machine knitting, wrapping the yarn is even easier. After you knit the short row and are ready to knit back, place the yarn into the hook of the next needle after the short row, then knit back. On a subsequent row, the extra loop of yarn will be knitted with the stitch on that needle, preventing a hole from forming at the turning point.

Fig. 62

Another way to short-row

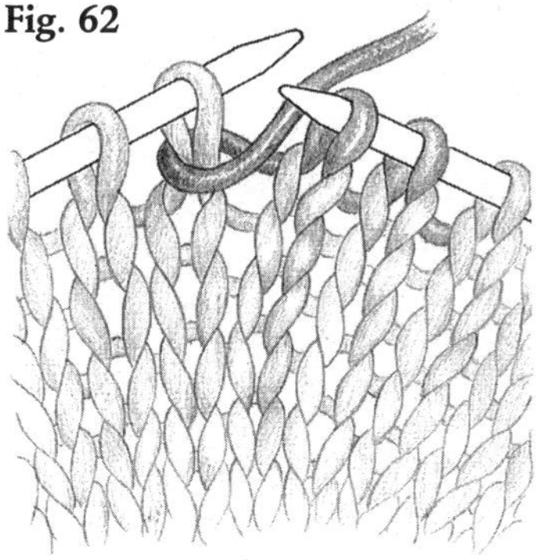

When ladies' sweaters are designed for large sizes, they should be worked with short-row bust darts, in progressively shorter rows across the front of the sweater. First, I decide how many stitches to leave unworked on the needle at the end of each row and for how many rows. Then all I do is work the short rows, turning with a yarn over. I always start short-rowing on the knit side and make my last short row on the purl side, which means that the first row I work to the end after the last short-row turn is a knit row. Here's how it works:

Knit the first short row, turn the work, and make a yarn over on the right needle and another yarn over to bring the yarn into position for purling. Purl the second short row, turn the work, and bring the yarn to the front. As you knit the first stitch of the next short row, you create the needed yarn over. After the last short-row turn, just knit each yarn over together with the next (lower) stitch as you come to them. On the purl side, just purling the yarn over together with the next stitch would put a twisted stitch on the front. So, instead, I interchange the yarn over with the next stitch: Take the right needle behind the yarn over and into the next purl stitch. Slip both off the left needle. Don't worry, the yarn over won't disappear. With the left needle, pick up the yarn over, then the stitch off the right needle. Then purl both together. When working a pattern stitch, work the pattern as far as possible, and turn. Coming back to the full row, work the pattern as need be from the center.

— *Renate Broeker, Memphis, TN*

BINDING OFF
Basic bind-off

The most popular method for binding off or casting off knit and purl stitches is to chain the stitches off the right needle one at a time. You accomplish this by first working two stitches, either knitting or purling to match the stitches in the row below. Then insert the left needle from left to right into the right stitch on the right needle, lift this stitch over the left stitch, and drop the right stitch off the needle. Knit or purl another stitch from the left needle and repeat the process with the two loops on the right needle, as shown in *Fig. 63*. Repeat across the row. When there is one stitch remaining, cut the yarn, leaving the end long if it's necessary for sewing, and pull the end through the remaining stitch.

Fig. 63

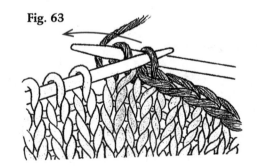

A quick bind-off

Binding off a piece of knitting can be difficult if the yarn is heavy or irregular or if the garment is bulky. You can save a lot of time and avoid frustration if you substitute a crochet hook approximately the same diameter as the knitting needle. Put the hook through the first loop on the left needle and knit the stitch onto the hook. Knit the next stitch onto the hook and pull the new stitch through the first one, as shown in *Fig. 64.* Continue in this manner to the end of the row and pull the yarn through the last loop on the hook. This takes me about a tenth of the time of a two-needle bind-off and makes a tight, even edge.

— *Lanette Scapillato, Issaquah, WA*

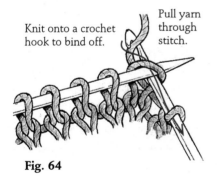

Knit onto a crochet hook to bind off.

Pull yarn through stitch.

Fig. 64

Stranded bind-off

The stranded bind-off is the simplest method of securing stitches. It performs the same function as the stranded cast-on (see pp. 19–20). You can also use it to temporarily hold stitches that will be picked up and worked later.

Cut the yarn end about a foot longer than the width of the knitting and thread a blunt tapestry needle. Beginning at the side that has the yarn end, slip the tapestry needle through several stitches on the knitting needle, as shown in *Fig. 65;* pull the yarn through, then drop the stitches off the knitting needle. Repeat across the row.

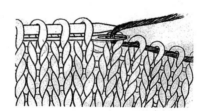

Fig. 65

A decorative ribbing bind-off

When I was completing a gansey that had employed a doubled-yarn cast-on and double rib (knit two, purl two), I wanted to finish the neck and sleeves with an attractive doubled-yarn bind-off that complemented the sweater's elaborate knit-purl patterns. The technique I developed produces a pretty braided edge that's very resistant to fraying. On the right side it looks like a braid of twined loops; underneath it has a firm, flat chain of knit V's.

At the beginning of the bind-off row, measure out a sufficiently long strand of yarn to knit together with the strand you're already using. Leave a tail in the new strand to weave into the wrong side, and purl the first two stitches with both strands held together as one. Pass the first stitch over the second. Continue purling one and passing the previous stitch over to the end of the round, and join the two ends to the first stitch. Then weave all three tails in on the wrong side. If you're knitting flat pieces, be sure to work this bind-off on the right side.

— *Alice DeCamp, Westport, CT*

Tubular bind-off for single rib

Once you learn this beautiful, stretchy bind-off that perfectly matches its cast-on counterpart, it will probably become your favorite. I call it the invisible bind-off. There are a few tricks in the way you think about the process that will make it easy. First, the yarn on the tapestry needle should always go under the knitting needle. Second, think about grafting the rib stitches as pairs: a pair of knits, then a pair of purls.

Work two rows of tubular stockinette stitch to begin the bind-off: For work beginning and ending with a knit stitch, knit one; then slip one purlwise with the yarn in front. Alternate these two stitches to the end of the row. On the second row, slip one purlwise with the yarn in front; then put the yarn to the back and knit one; repeat these two steps to the end of the row.

If your first stitch is a knit, the knits will be on the front layer, and the purls will be on the back. Starting the bind-off is a little tricky, but once you've entered the first two stitches the first time, you can work in pairs from then on, and a pleasant rhythm develops. Break off a length of yarn about four times as long as the edge you're binding off, and thread a blunt tapestry needle on the end. Hold the work with the right side facing you.

Step 1: The beginning stitches: Insert the tapestry needle into the first knit stitch as if to purl. Pull the yarn through and leave the stitch on the knitting needle. Working around from the back, bring the needle to the front between the knit stitch and the next purl stitch, and insert it into the first purl stitch as if to knit; it's tricky, and it looks as if you're twisting the front leg of the stitch when the needle exits toward the left *(Fig. 66)*. Pull the yarn through, leaving the stitch on the knitting needle. Both of the stitches are still on the needle.

Step 2: Work the pairs of knit stitches as follows, remembering that a stitch isn't dropped until the tapestry needle has passed through it twice: Insert the needle knitwise back into the first knit stitch and drop it. Don't pull the yarn through yet. Insert the needle purlwise into the next knit stitch (third stitch). Leave it on the knitting needle and pull the yarn through *(Fig. 67)*. This completes the work for a pair of knit stitches. Only the first stitch of the pair has been dropped; the second stitch will become the first stitch of the next knit pair.

Step 3: Each pair of purl stitches is worked as follows: Slip the first purl stitch off onto the tapestry needle, as if to purl, but don't pull the yarn through. Loop the yarn to the right and under the knitting needle toward the back. Then insert the needle from the back into the next purl stitch knitwise, as described above. Both of these steps are shown in *Fig. 68*. Pull the yarn through, being careful not to pull it too tightly.

Continue grafting pairs of knits and pairs of purls in this manner until you reach the end of the row. Notice that you always insert the tapestry needle into the first stitch of the pair the way you would knit that type of stitch—knitwise into the first knit, purlwise into the first purl—and that this stitch is always dropped. The second stitch of the pair is worked in the opposite manner, and the tapestry needle is always passed out and away from the work.

If the first stitch of the rib is a purl, reverse the order of the tubular rows and the stitches in step 1. Then start working at step 3.

— *Betty J. Louie, Carmichael, CA*

Fig. 66

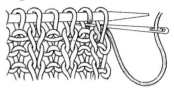

Insert needle purlwise into first knit stitch and knitwise from behind into first purl stitch. Leave both stitches on needle.

Fig. 67

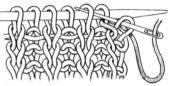

For a pair of knit stitches, insert needle knitwise into first knit stitch and drop it. Then go purlwise into second knit stitch.

Fig. 68

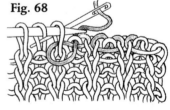

Go purlwise into first purl stitch and drop it. Loop yarn to right and under knitting needle and insert tapestry needle knitwise from back into second purl stitch.

Tubular bind-off for double rib

The process of binding off a tubular double rib is similar to the process of binding off a tubular single rib, although there are nearly twice as many steps.

Work two tubular rows to begin: Knit the first knit stitch of each rib and slip the second purlwise with the yarn in back; purl the first purl stitch and slip the second purlwise with the yarn in front. Two things are crucial for a successful tubular double-rib bind-off:

Fig. 69

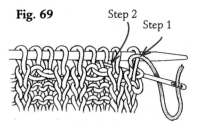

Insert needle purlwise into first knit stitch (step 1). Then, working from back and under knitting needle, insert needle knitwise into first purl stitch (step 2).

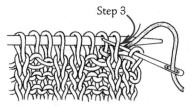

Insert needle knitwise into first knit stitch, looping yarn over top of stitch, and drop it. Then insert needle purlwise into second knit stitch (step 3).

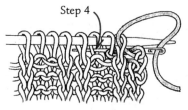

Loop yarn up and, working in back from right to left, insert needle purlwise into first purl stitch, then knitwise into second purl stitch (step 4).

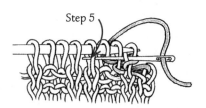

Insert needle knitwise into second knit stitch and drop it. Insert needle purlwise into third knit stitch (step 5) and drop first purl stitch.

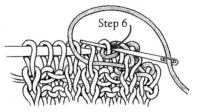

Insert needle purlwise into second purl stitch and drop it (step 6).

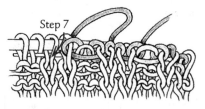

Working around from back, insert needle knitwise into third purl stitch (step 7). Repeat from step 3.

Work around the back knitwise into the purl stitches, just the way you did for the single rib. Also, to avoid twisting the tops of the stitches, be very careful to loop the yarn and insert the needle as shown. *Fig. 69* shows a ribbing that begins with two knit stitches.

Avoid going twice into the first two stitches

In tubular bind-off, it's best not to get into the habit of going twice into the first two stitches. First, it isn't strictly necessary. Second, the tubular bind-off is often used to finish necklines worked in rounds. In this case, the last two stitches become the right-hand neighbors of the first two stitches. If you've gone only into the first two stitches, you can go into them a second time at the end of the binding-off sequence and link them to the last two stitches. This gives a totally undetectable join. If you have already gone twice into the first two stitches, you'll have a problem unless, of course, you started to bind off by linking the first two stitches directly with the last two stitches. *See Figs. 70–72.*

— *Montse Stanley, Cambridge, England*

Another technique for tubular bind-off, double rib

I've found an easy way to work tubular bind-off for knit two, purl two rib. First I transfer the purl stitches onto a double-pointed needle and hold it behind and parallel to the needle with the knit stitches. For work beginning with knit two, I treat the first knit stitch as a purl stitch and slip it onto the back needle, as shown in *Fig. 73.*

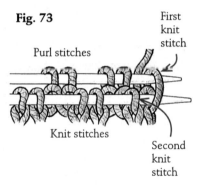

Fig. 73

Purl stitches

First knit stitch

Knit stitches

Second knit stitch

Transfer purl stitches to double-pointed needle held behind knit stitches. Treat first knit as a purl to begin tubular bind-off of double rib.

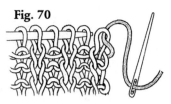

Fig. 70

Insert needle knitwise into first (knit) stitch and drop it. The first time around you go into this stitch only once.

Fig. 71

Insert needle purlwise into third (knit) stitch, then purlwise into second (purl) stitch. Drop second stitch. The first time around, you go into it only once.

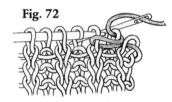

Fig. 72

Insert needle knitwise into fourth (purl) stitch, from back. Repeat from beginning.

Hand-Knitting Techniques 55

I bind off with the same steps I would use for tubular bind-off, single rib (see pp. 53–54). I begin by inserting from the back into the first stitch on the back needle (knit treated as purl) as if to knit. Then I go into the first stitch on the front needle (second knit) as if to purl. These two stitches remain on their needles, and I work a pair of purls: Slip the first purl off purlwise (the first time this stitch is the knit treated as a purl), then go into the second purl from the back knitwise. Then I work a pair of knits: Slip the first knit off knitwise, then go purlwise into the second knit. Continue in this rhythm—a pair of purls from the back needle, then a pair of knits from the front needle—to the end of the row.

— *Betty J. Louie, Carmichael, CA*

One-row flat-chain bind-off

You might want to try my method for a one-row flat-chain bind-off as an alternative to Montse Stanley's decrease bind-off. I feel that the smoother edge of this version is more desirable than Stanley's crochetlike finish. On single rib, beginning with a knit stitch, *purl two together and leave the stitch on the right needle. Carry the yarn to the back, knit one, and pass the first stitch on the right needle over it. Bring the yarn forward, transfer the stitch from the right needle back to the left needle, and repeat from * to the end of the row.

Work the one-row flat-chain bind-off for double rib as follows for work beginning knit two: Knit two, pass the first knit stitch over the second knit stitch. [Bring the yarn forward. *Transfer the stitch from the right needle to the left needle. Purl two together. Repeat from * once. Carry the yarn back. **Knit one, pass the first stitch on the right needle over. Repeat from ** once.] Repeat between [ ] to the end of the row.

— *Betty J. Louie, Carmichael, CA*

To bind off loosely

Whenever a knitting pattern says "bind off loosely," I switch to a needle three sizes larger than the size I've been using for the pattern. I find this much easier than changing my tension, and the results are perfectly even.

— *Jennifer Lobb, Lynden, ONT, Canada*

Slipped-stitch bind-off

To prevent an enlarged loop at the end of a bound-off row, try this: On the last row before the bind-off row, slip the first stitch as if to purl, then work to the end of the row. Turn and bind off.

— *Leslie Calaway, Roseville, CA*

RIPPING OUT AND PICKING UP STITCHES
Picking up a dropped stitch

Dropping a stitch is often unintentional, although there are a couple of interesting pattern stitches that rely on dropped stitches for their effect, such as needle weaving

when combined with knitting. If you've accidentally dropped a stitch in the row you're currently knitting, rip out the stitches until you get back to the dropped offender. Carefully move the old stitches back to the left needle so they are correctly positioned and match the other stitches on that needle *(Fig. 74)*. Pick up the dropped stitch, position it on the left needle like the other stitches, and work the stitch.

If you dropped a stitch several rows below the one you're currently working, a ladder will have formed. Use a crochet hook to work the stitch up the ladder, rung by rung. To correct a knit stitch, insert the hook into the stitch from the front *(Fig. 75)*; to correct a purl stitch, insert the hook into the stitch from the back *(Fig. 76)*. When you reach the top row, correctly position the stitch on the left needle to knit or purl.

Fig. 74

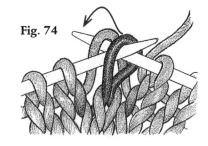

Fig. 75

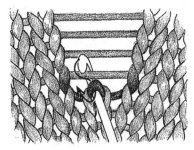

Fig. 76

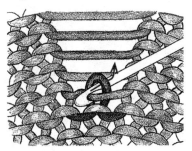

Ripping stockinette stitch

To rip back many rows in stockinette stitch, take a thinner needle and run it under the front leg of every stitch on the row below the mistake, as shown in *Fig. 77*. Then just rip away. The ripping stops when you get to the needle, and all the stitches are set correctly so you can resume knitting after transferring them to the right-size needle. Since I always use circular needles, either end is ready to knit.

—*Peg Boren, McAllen, TX*

Fig. 77

Slip needle through front leg of each stitch on row so ripping will stop with stitches aligned.

Fig. 78

Picking up loose stitches

Knitters often need to pick up stitches that are off the needles. This happens most commonly in hand knitting because you've dropped a few stitches or have taken the work off the needles to rip (unravel) several rows. Machine knitters often rip out a waste-yarn machine cast-on to free the bottom-edge stitches and complete a sweater by hand.

If you plan to start knitting with a new ball of yarn, you can pick up with either the knit or purl side facing you. Slip the needle into the loose loops from right to left and back to front, as shown in *Fig. 78*. The first row will be worked on the other side. However, if you're picking up after ripping a few rows, and the tip of the left needle needs to end up at the right edge, where the ball is already attached, slip the needle in from left to right and front to back so the last stitch you pick up is at the ball. You can pick up with either the knit or purl side facing you, and your first row will be on the same side.

Your goal is always to pick up the stitches so they aren't twisted, because if you knit a twisted stitch in the normal manner, it will be tighter than the other stitches and, being crossed at the bottom, it will look different.

To tell whether the loops are twisted or not is easy: The stitch is untwisted on the left needle if it opens wide when you insert the right needle to knit or purl (drawing 1, *Fig. 79*). But if it crosses at the base when you insert the right needle into it (drawing 2, *Fig. 79*), it was picked up backward (twisted). Replace it on the left needle or knit it by passing the right needle through the half of the stitch loop on the back side of the left needle (drawing 3, *Fig. 79*) to untwist it.

Picking up stitches

Pick up stitches for attaching a knitted cord such as I-cord by inserting the pick-up needle through both sides of a stitch in a column

and pulling a loop through, as shown in *Fig. 80*. Repeat, working down the column, for the desired number of stitches.

ODDS AND ENDS
When it hurts, stop and look

In my experience, carpal tunnel problems usually can be traced to improper technique. I played violin for 20 years, six years as a full-time professional. Fortunately, my first violin teacher warned me of the possibilities of permanent injury and gave me the following advice:

If it hurts, stop. Pain is your body's way of telling you that something is wrong. Do not continue your activity in the hope that the pain will go away. After the pain stops, analyze what you were doing when the pain started. Pay particular attention to stress in your neck, shoulders, elbows, wrists, and hands. Correct your technique so that it is closer to your body's natural movements. If you stand in front of a mirror with your arms hanging completely relaxed from your shoulders, you'll notice that your

Fig. 79

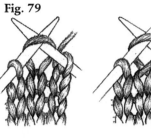

1. Correct (not twisted) 2. Twisted

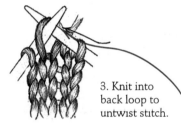

3. Knit into back loop to untwist stitch.

Fig. 80

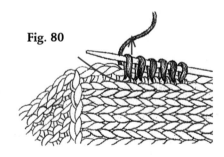

wrists are straight, with your fingers slightly curved toward your palms. Try to use this natural position as a base for your activity. Experiment gently until you find a relaxed position for your arms and hands that will eliminate strain, discomfort, or pain. Your position may feel awkward at first, but remember how awkward you felt the first time you picked up knitting needles or a crochet hook!

Try to remain sensitive to any strain in your body. These are some of the most common problems I've observed:

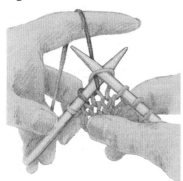

Fig. 81

- Raising one or both shoulders. The shoulders can creep up gradually if you are under stress.
- Sticking one or both elbows out sideways. Try to keep your elbows closer to your body.
- Sticking your wrist out in unnatural directions.
- Letting your body become locked into a single position for long periods of time. Shift your position frequently.

I tend to cock my right wrist sideways when I knit. As soon as I feel the slightest twinge of pain, I know it's time to take a short break. When I start again, I pay extra attention to the position of my right arm and hand. It seems a small price to pay for ensuring that I'll be able to enjoy knitting for many years to come!

— *Denise Jackson, San Francisco, CA*

Leftward knitting for rightward knitters

Leftward knitting isn't just for lefties. Have you ever complained about having to constantly turn your knitting to work the few stitches of a bobble before resuming a row? I've discovered what many knitters already know: You don't have to turn the work, and you don't have to purl the wrong-side rows of bobbles. Merely knit them leftward.

Since the stitches have just been knit rightward, they'll be twisted for the leftward row. Here's how to keep the fabric untwisted and have the stitches oriented properly on the next rightward row: On leftward rows, enter the stitch as shown in *Fig. 81,* but bring the yarn from behind, over the left needle, then under and away. Alternate right and left knitting for the required number of rows, bind off the bobble stitches, and keep going.

You can use this method for short-rowing, too. The only problem you'll have is that at first your leftward tension will be different from your normal rightward tension, but practice should correct this.

When you're knitting complicated color patterns on flat pieces, you'll find it harder to strand and keep to the pattern on the purl side because you can't see the pattern clearly. Knit the purl rows in a leftward direction, and the right side will always face you. I'm no longer a skeptic. Leftward knitting is great for all knitters.

— *Alice Korach*

Knitting backward

Knitting backward is helpful when you're knitting narrow areas, bobbles, or short rows, which would otherwise require frequent turning of the work back and forth to knit the right side and purl the wrong side. When knitting backward, you can knit faster by working every row from the right side, without turning at the end of a row. Knitting backward also makes it easier to follow a graphed design, because you don't have to

Fig. 82

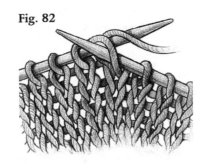

reverse every other row of the graph, as you would if purling from the wrong side.

To knit backward at the end of a knit row and keep the stitches untwisted and properly oriented for the next knit row, insert the left needle from front to back into the first stitch on the right needle. Wrap the yarn from left to right over the left needle, and pull the wrap through the loop, as shown in *Fig. 82*. Alternate a row of forward and a row of backward knitting as needed to complete the required section.

Thimbles for knitters

Knitting small stitches on small, sharp needles? Slip on a leather quilting thimble. It protects fingertips while maintaining feel and flexibility.

— *Margaret Rauhut, Chicago, IL*

THREE

MULTICOLOR KNITTING

Stranded Knitting

Intarsia Knitting

Other Color
Techniques

Bobbin Basics

Odds and Ends

STRANDED KNITTING

Stranded weaving

Stranded weaving is a way to carry a yarn at the back when knitting Fair Isle or stranded knitting, without creating long floats between areas of the same color. You simply twist the two yarns together every two or three stitches, using a loose, even tension.

Single-handed two-color knitting

There are several techniques for holding the yarns when knitting with two colors in a row. Here is a method in which both colors are held in the same hand: The first strand (A) is held in the right hand as if you were knitting with it alone, with the yarn passing over the index finger and under the palm of the hand. The second strand (B), closest to you, is held between the thumb and the index or middle finger and also passes under the palm. As you knit, throw whichever color is called for in the pattern. To throw A, raise your index finger and wrap the needle, as shown in *Fig. 83*. To throw B, rotate your hand clockwise so that the palm is more visible, and pick up B with your index finger so you can wrap the needle *(Fig. 84)*. For even knitting, always hold the same color in the same position in your hand.

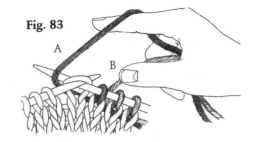

Fig. 83

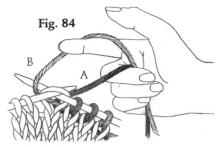

Fig. 84

Two-handed two-color knitting

I have always used and taught the "two-fisted" system of stranded knitting, with one color held in each hand: the right-hand color thrown American style, and the left-hand color picked in the Continental way. This is wonderfully rhythmic and easy to do on the knit side. Even weaving in of either color to avoid long floats is quickly learned. However, American-style knitters have a terrible time purling with the left hand, and we end up with a tangled mess of yarn and uneven knitting when we do stranded knitting in the flat.

The solution is to put one color around the neck. From the knitting, the yarn goes

Fig. 85

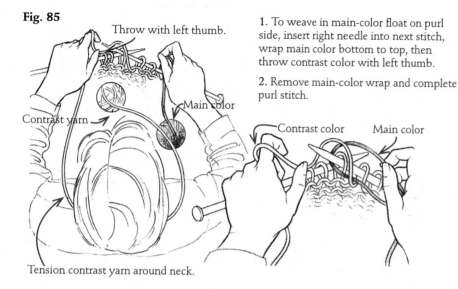

Throw with left thumb.

Contrast yarn

Main color

Tension contrast yarn around neck.

1. To weave in main-color float on purl side, insert right needle into next stitch, wrap main color bottom to top, then throw contrast color with left thumb.

2. Remove main-color wrap and complete purl stitch.

Contrast color   Main color

over the left shoulder, around the neck, and down over the right shoulder. The right-hand color is purled with the right hand as usual. When the left color is called for, you just flip it over the needle with the left thumb, as shown in the left drawing of *Fig. 85.* I seldom have a tension problem, but with a slippery yarn it is easy to loop the yarn through the fingers of the right hand. Moving your head back or lowering your hands can counteract left-hand slack.

To weave in the contrasting color, if the main color is needed for more than three or four stitches, hold the contrasting yarn up with the thumb and purl one stitch with the main color under it. Work the next few stitches as usual with the right hand, and the yarn will naturally be thrown over the neck yarn.

If the pattern calls for a run of contrasting color, weave in the main color by purling with the contrasting color and the flip method for two stitches. Then put the needle in the next stitch, and wrap the right-hand yarn from bottom to top. Do not purl the stitch, just wrap. Flip the left yarn as usual. Remove the right-hand wrap, as shown in the right drawing of *Fig. 85,* and complete the stitch.

I have found that I can purl Fair Isle work using this method just as fast and smoothly as I can knit it—not counting the time it takes to explain what I'm doing to amused bystanders.

— *Sandy Terp, Phillipsburg, NJ*

Stranding effortlessly—almost

Classic stranded knitting requires that you carry one strand in each hand. Like any technique, this takes some getting used to.

I always put the background color in my left hand, my preferred knitting method, and the pattern color in my right, since it's generally used a little less. This way, when I'm reading a chart as I knit, I automatically throw all the pattern stitches with the yarn in my right hand. I recommend that you learn to knit with the method that you don't normally use: English/American if you knit Continental, or Continental if you knit English/American. It shouldn't take you more than a few hours of feeling awkward, which is a small price to pay for a very rewarding and quick technique—two-hand stranded knitting.

— *Alice Korach*

High-speed Fair Isle

Many knitters are attracted to multicolored patterns in which the unused yarns are stranded behind the work, but they are discouraged by the slow pace of the work when changing colors repeatedly across each row. Here's a speedy alternative to the typical process: Using either circular or double-pointed needles, work across the row, knitting every stitch that should be in color A and slipping (as if to purl) every stitch that should be in color B, which you can ignore for the time being. At the end of the row and without turning, slide the stitches back to the right point of the needle, pick up color B, drop A, and work every stitch that should be B, slipping every stitch that was previously worked in A. Now you can turn and work the same way on the purl side. If you're working in the round, knit one round with A, then one round with B to complete each single row. Besides providing a considerable increase in speed, you'll find this method makes it easier than usual to control the tension of the strands, avoiding gathered, rippling fabric. After you slip a group of stitches, stretch them out smoothly on the right needle before stranding the yarn past to the next stitch. This will measure out just the right amount of yarn for that strand.

— *June Hemmons Hiatt, San Francisco, CA*

Back-and-forth knitting

The simplest Fair Isle patterns require working simultaneously with two balls of yarn. Argyle and complex contemporary patterns may require several balls. The secret to changing colors in the middle of a row without leaving a hole in the work is to tightly twist the new yarn around the old. Sounds great. But this simple twist at every color change, coupled with turning the work around at the end of a row, quickly makes a mess of strands that would cause Arachne to shudder!

The solution is to knit back and forth on the same side of the fabric, no matter what kind of stitch you're making. (This technique is also useful when you're making a large, heavy, or bulky item that is difficult to turn after every row.)

To visualize the technique, loosely knit about 1 inch of a 20-stitch stockinette swatch, changing colors in the row. When you get to the end of a knit row, stop. In stockinette, you'd normally turn the work to purl the back. But purling is simply knitting on the wrong side, so, although you'll be working on the front side of the fabric, you'll be making the same stitch you'd be making if you were purling on the back side. You'll be working from the left edge of the fabric to the right, instead of from right to left. Insert the left-needle tip into the back of the first stitch on the right needle, slipping the

left needle behind the right. (To check the needle's position, turn your work around and insert the needle as if to purl; then look at it on the wrong side.) Wrap the working yarn around the left-needle tip counterclockwise *(Fig. 86),* and pull the left-needle tip through the space underneath the right needle to form the stitch.

When knitting from left needle to right, the twists at the color changes are all counterclockwise. When you knit back across the row, from right needle to left, the color changes are twisted clockwise. By the time

Fig. 86

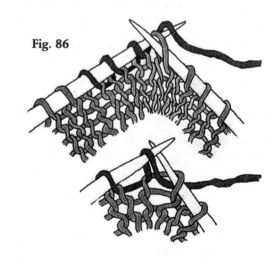

66

you get to the end of the row, all of your yarns are untangled and ready to go again for the next row.

— *Shelley Cypher, Laguna Niguel, CA*

Managing twisted knitting yarns

Instructions for multicolor knitting usually tell you to pick up a new color from under the old color, which twists the yarns. If your colors are wound onto bobbins, and you're working back and forth on two needles, the strands are not hard to untwist. However, I prefer to work straight from the ball and in the round, so the yarns twist more and more as I work. As soon as the twists become awkward, I start picking up the new color from over the old color, and the yarns start to untwist. When the yarns are fully untwisted, I switch back to picking up under the old color, and the problem takes care of itself. I also put the balls of yarn into a bag or box a few feet away from me. This seems to extend the amount of time I can twist the yarns in one direction.

— *Debbie Ott, Glenella, MB, Canada*

No-bunch stranding

Many people fear stranded knitting because they're sure that they'll produce "seersucker." The trick to keeping the knitting flat and tension even is remarkably simple: Don't let the stitches you've knit pile up near the tip of your right needle. Just keep smoothing and spreading them out along the needle as you go. You can crowd the left-needle stitches as much as you like, without dropping them. If you get into the habit of spreading the just-knit stitches to their correct gauge width, particularly as you carry the new color behind them to begin using it, your floats will be exactly the right length—neither long and sloppy, nor too tight—and your knit fabric will be perfectly flat.

— *Alice Korach*

INTARSIA KNITTING
Basic intarsia

Knitting with the intarsia method is one way to knit with several colors. Unlike stranded knitting, where the colors are knitted in frequently along the row and carried across

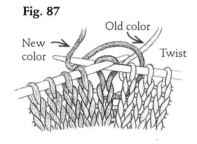

Fig. 87

New color

Old color

Twist

the back of the fabric when not in use, the colors in intarsia knitting generally appear at isolated spots along the row, as shown in *Fig. 87,* and each color of yarn is left hanging until needed in the next row, when it's picked up and knitted. Intarsia produces a single thickness of fabric, whereas stranded knitting creates a double- or triple-thick fabric, depending on the number of colors that are used.

Twist yarns at the color change when you're knitting intarsia or argyle to prevent holes from forming between colors. Whether knitting or purling, the new color yarn is always positioned to the right of the old color yarn. Drop the color you've just finished and, with your right hand, reach under it for the new color, as shown in *Fig. 88*. If the new color is already to the right of the old color, i.e., you've knit past it with the color you're about to drop, just knit or purl without twisting. It will automatically cross over the color change place, so no hole will form.

If you forget to twist on the one-stitch crosshatching in argyle knitting, the crosshatched stitches will be crossed rather than flat.

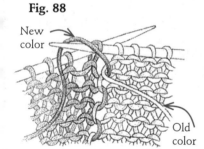

Fig. 88

New color

Old color

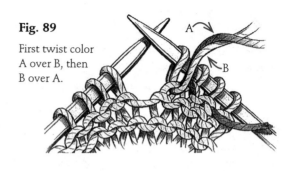

Fig. 89

First twist color A over B, then B over A.

A

B

To add a new color in intarsia and finish the yarn end at the same time, twist in the new yarn with the three stitches just before the new yarn is needed. Hold the new color yarn at the back of the work and wrap the yarns together between each of the three stitches before the color change, as shown in *Fig. 89*. To keep tangling to a minimum, alternate the direction of the twist on adjacent stitches.

Getting the upper hand on intarsia

Twisting the yarns: Different books describe the technique of twisting the yarns at each color change to prevent holes differently, but if you study the pictures, they all boil down to the same thing: Intarsia knitting is really ideal for people who prefer to carry the yarn in the right hand. This is because when you finish knitting (or purling) with a color, you just drop it and reach under it with your right hand to take up the next color. This simple action puts a half twist between the yarns when you knit the next stitch because it brings the new color around, to the right, and over the old color, as shown in *Fig. 90*. If the new yarn is already on the right-hand side of the old color (because you knit past it), just pick it up and knit with it; there won't be a hole. Knitters who hold the yarn in their left hand will need to pick up the new color with their right hand and transfer it to the left hand.

Preparing the colors: Every separate occurrence of every color in intarsia knitting requires its own little ball. Here's how to determine the approximate lengths you'll need for each design element in your pattern as you knit your patterned gauge swatch: For each color or pattern element in the 6-inch or larger swatch, tie a knot every yard. Then, as you knit, count the number of knots you pass and multiply that by 36; subtract the length that remains to the next knot from 36, and add it to the previous number.

But don't cut all the lengths before you need them: If you're knitting with different kinds of yarn, thicker ones will require somewhat more length and thinner ones somewhat less than your average gauge swatch indicated. I always add a selvage stitch at each edge on every piece so that the design won't be affected by seaming: these extra stitches will also require extra length. Besides, you might want to change your pattern or color while you're knitting.

I usually wind my premeasured yarn lengths into butterflies to keep them from tangling (see the drawing below). These small center-pull skeins make handling the many

Fig. 90

Drop old color and reach under it with right hand for new color, whether knitting or purling. This connects the yarns with half a twist, preventing a hole between them.

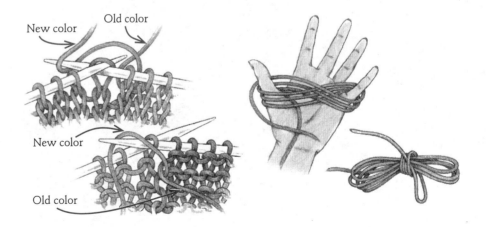

New color
Old color
New color
Old color

lengths of yarn in an intarsia sweater much easier than just letting the yarn ends dangle, unless the lengths are very short.

— *Nancy Marchant*

Seamless intarsia

I've discovered an easy way to knit seamless garments with several colors in intarsia. Multicolor knitting in the round is generally perceived to be impossible because after the first row has been knit around, the yarn for

Fig. 91

Turning point; make initial twist here.

Knit direction

You are here.

Loop

Skein for last color in row

Pass skein through loop when you get to last color.

each color change ends up on the wrong side of the color area, instead of at the beginning, where you need it for the next row. The solution is to purl every other row as you would with straight needles, always turning at a color change.

In order to keep your knitting a seamless tube while you're working back and forth, you twist the first and last colors together before you begin each next row. When you reach the last color area, pass the skein for the color you just finished through the loop made by the initial twist, as shown in *Fig. 91*. You'll then purl or knit the remaining stitches using yarn from the loop (which of course slides freely in the initial twist), then slide the loop closed at the end of the row.

When the color change is on a diagonal, as in argyles, simply slip a stitch or two at the end of a round in order to maintain the pattern. This technique can be used with as many colors as you like, for virtually any intarsia pattern, including seamless argyle socks.

— *Nancy Larson, Knoxville, TN*

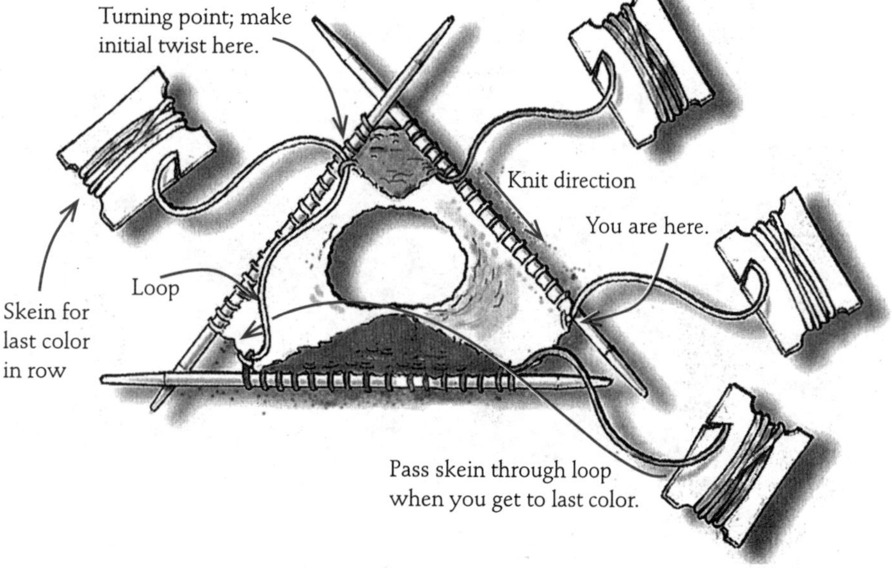

Invisible intarsia ends

One knitter who works for me likes to weave in all her ends around the carried-up threads with a crochet hook or tapestry needle when the knitting is finished, as shown in *Fig. 94,* but most knitters find finishing easier if they've already knit in all the starting ends of each color. To ensure the invisibility of woven-in ends, I try to weave them in only on top of their own color, which means that not all starting ends can be knit in into the first row, and all finishing ends must be woven in by hand later. I keep a crochet hook one size smaller than the knitting needles I'm using in my basket so that whenever I feel like it, I can stop knitting and relax a bit by weaving in ends. If there's intarsia in the ribbing, you need to weave in those ends a little more securely so you can cut the tails short.

Figs. 92, 93, 95, and *96* show different methods to begin and knit in ends. There are several variables you need to deal with: Will you have several stitches of the new color behind which the end can be woven on its first row *(Fig. 92)*? Or will you have only one stitch? In that case, you must weave

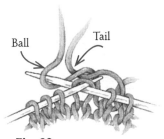

Fig. 92

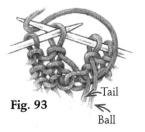

Fig. 93

Fig. 94

Beginning a New Color of Several Stitches

To knit first stitch, lay the new color yarn around right needle with tail hanging between needles. Knit first stitch of new color, leaving 2" tail. Insert right needle to knit next stitch, bring tail under, then over old color and new color, then wrap new color and knit (this crosses tail once and prevents hole between colors). Bring new color under tail to cross it when knitting third stitch, then over tail for fourth. Tail is now woven in. Leave at least ½" hanging in back so it won't peek through.

Beginning a New Color With One Stitch

Weave tail in over several rows, crossing tail in when you twist threads in a color change and carrying tail up knitting. Weave tail in toward direction it came from to keep first stitch from twisting when you knit stitch above it.

Weaving in Ends With a Crochet Hook

To prevent hole, hook thread first into carried thread of color next to or above its own color. Then hook thread through and around carried threads of its own color along color-change line.

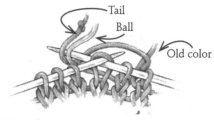

Fig. 95

Beginning a Slippery Yarn

Tie fat knot in end. Knit first stitch. Cross tail
under old color, then pick up both tail and new
color together and knit next stitch with both ends.
Cross tail with new color for next 2 to 3 stitches,
as shown here. On next row, treat double-thread
stitch as a single-thread stitch. After weaving in
final end, tie fat knot in it as well.

Fig. 96

Beginning a Thin Yarn

Knit first stitch of new color as usual. Work next
2 to 3 stitches with both ends of new color. On
next row, treat double-thread stitches as if they
were single-thread stitches.

the tail up the side of the new color area
as you twist yarns for the color change
(Fig. 93). Weave the tail along the side at
which it exits the first stitch. Is the yarn
hairy or textured so that it will stay where
it is put? Or is it slippery so that weaving
it in requires a bit more care *(Fig. 95)*? And
finally, is the yarn thinner or thicker than its
fellows? If it's thin, you can use the doubled
stitch method shown in *Fig. 96,* which is the
easiest weaving-in technique but often adds
too much bulk.

— *Nancy Marchant*

Purl duplicate stitch for intarsia ends

Purl duplicate stitch is a very neat and secure
method for weaving in the many ends of
yarn that result with intarsia (knitting with
many yarn colors in short pieces). Working
on the wrong side, thread the colored yarn
end onto a tapestry needle. Then insert the
needle into the closest adjacent purl bump
along the lower half of the same row as the
colored stitch from which the tail exits, going
away from the colored stitches *(Fig. 97)*. This
bump curves downward, like a frown. Follow
the thread path and insert the needle into

the bump just above; this stitch is connected to the edge colored stitch. It curves up like a smile. Weave under about four pairs of purl bumps, always going through each twice and moving away from the intarsia block to close up the hole between colors.

OTHER COLOR TECHNIQUES
Adventures in color blending

You can achieve a blended color effect by knitting alternate stitches in two shades of the same color. Reverse the position of the colors on each succeeding row to prevent

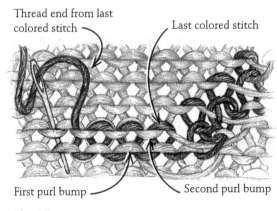

Thread end from last colored stitch

Last colored stitch

First purl bump

Second purl bump

Fig. 97

vertical stripes. Alternate the colors by carrying the nonknitting color behind the knitting color every stitch. This creates a subtle texture.

Color blending, take two

Because I don't dye my own yarns, I used to feel limited by the colors that were available from yarn companies. Wanting to incorporate subtle color shading into my garments, I discovered that knitting with two or more strands of fine yarn held together allows me to change one strand at a time and get intermediate, blended shades.
— *Gillian Bull*

One-row stripes in flat knitting

When you want to randomize the patches produced by variegated yarn or different dye lots, use up assorted colors, or change gradually from one color to another, try knitting with three balls of yarn, changing yarns at the end of every row. The floats of yarn will be short and inconspicuous, and both edges will be the same. Three closely related colors in garter stitch give a tweed

Fig. 98

Contrast color appears alternately
on the right and wrong sides.

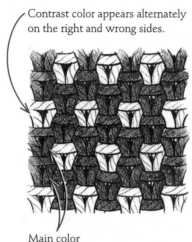

Main color

effect. Two balls of the main color and one
ball of a contrast color worked in hopsac, or
woven, stitch produce polka dots *(Fig. 98)*.
Work hopsac stitch on an odd number of
stitches, repeating two rows as follows:

Row 1:

K1, *sl 1 pwise with yarn in front, k1*,
rep to end of row.

Row 2:

P2, *sl 1 pwise with yarn in back, p1*,
rep to end of row.

— *Joy Beeson, Voorheesville, NY*

Reversible sweaters

I love to make many-colored sweaters
inspired by Kaffe Fassett, and have recog-
nized that the inside is often as attractive, in
a handwoven sort of way, as the outside. So
I've started making reversible sweaters. The
two sides look very different, so I feel like I
get two sweaters instead of one.

To make the sweater reversible, I knit
with floats that extend all the way to the
selvage, even when that isn't necessary to the
"front" pattern. I weave in the ends carefully,
join neatly, and make ribbings or hems that
are attractive on the back as well as the front.
Pockets in the side seams are no problem at
all; they just turn inside out. To make the
buttons reversible, I knit buttonholes on both
sides of the front. Then I sew the buttons to
a length of grosgrain ribbon and button them
through the side where they would usually
be sewn. Then I can button the other side
over them. When I turn the sweater inside
out, I just unbutton the ribbon and button it
through the other side, which also makes the
sweater unisex.

— *Lynn Derus, Atlanta, GA*

Reversible knitting

About 10 years ago, I came across a knitted afghan pattern in a craft magazine that used a stitch I hadn't seen before: a double stitch that made the afghan reversible. Intrigued, I tried a swatch. The technique was fun and fast, and I was hooked. The trick of the double stitch is that you're working two layers of fabric, each in two colors, in every row. That is, while you're knitting jade green flowers on a black background, you're also knitting black flowers on jade green on the reverse side.

Picking yarns: Finding the right yarn is extremely important because this double stitch is too heavy for garments in some yarns. For instance, worsted-weight yarn makes wonderful double-knit afghans, but it's too bulky for garments. You'll have the best results with a finer yarn and smaller needles. However, even when you use smaller needles, this stitch tends to spread. For example, if you want to make a pattern that calls for a worsted-weight gauge of 5 stitches per inch, you'll achieve that gauge with sport-weight yarn (which normally knits at about 6 stitches per inch). And if you want to get 6 stitches per inch in a reversible garment, you'll need to go to a fingering- or baby-weight yarn.

Yarns that are tightly twisted also add undesirable weight to garments. The best bets are soft, lightweight yarns with a loose twist. A fluffy yarn with mohair works well, too. I've had good results with washable acrylic/wool blends for children's sweaters and hats.

Picking patterns: You can adapt patterns you already have to double knitting. However, as mentioned before, the double-stitch gauge will be completely different from the recommended gauge for that yarn. So here are my guidelines for swatching: Start with two colors in a yarn you love. Experimenting with needle sizes, make swatches until you get a fabric you like. Measure the gauge of your swatch, only counting the stitches on one side. Then find a pattern to match the stitch-per-inch gauge you've achieved. The double stitch works up more squat than most other stitches, so your row count probably won't match the pattern's at all. But that's okay, because you can work additional rows until you get the

Double-Knitting Basics

Yarn A   Yarn B

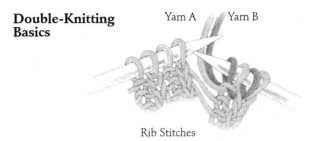

Rib Stitches

How to start double-knitting from ribbing: In each rib stitch, knit with yarn A, holding both yarns to the back. With the new stitch on the right needle, bring both yarns to the front and purl with yarn B in the original stitch on the left needle, then slip the stitch to the right needle. This doubles the number of stitches and sets up the two-faced fabric.

Working the back layer: With both yarns held to the front, purl the purl stitch.

Working the front layer: With both yarns held to the back, knit the knit stitch.

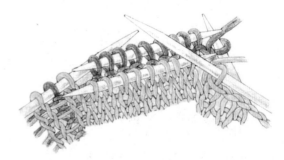

Bind off each side separately: Slip the stitches from the front layer and from the back to separate double-pointed needles. Bind off the first stitches knitwise and purlwise. You may do this in sections, as shown here.

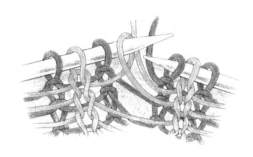

Increase on each layer separately: Lift and twist the strand between the knit stitches as shown here and, with both yarns in back, knit one stitch. Lift and twist the strand between the purl stitches and, with both yarns in front, purl one stitch. This increases one stitch in each layer.

Holding pin or cable needle

Decrease on each layer separately: Slip a knit stitch from the left needle onto the right needle. Slip a purl stitch to a holding pin and return the knit stitch to the left needle as shown. With both yarns in back, knit two knit stitches together. Place the purl stitch on the holding pin back on the left needle. With both yarns in front, purl the two stitches together.

length, in inches, that you need. However, make sure that the double stitches don't distort two-color patters, such as Fair Isle, by squashing the design too much.

— *M'Lou Linsert Baber*

Adding color motifs after the knitting is done

There are two ways to add color to a piece after the work is finished. Swiss darning, or duplicate stitch, allows you to completely cover plain stockinette, forming a motif over the knitting *(Fig. 99)*. The stitches will look slightly larger and somewhat raised as compared to the uncovered knit stitches. For large motifs, work Swiss darning in blocks of stitches. Work from right to left to the end of the first row, turn the work upside down, and work the second row from right to left also. You can also cross-stitch directly onto stockinette-stitch fabric, using one cross-stitch for each knit stitch, as shown in *Fig. 100*.

—*Wendy Keele*

Fig. 99

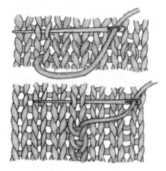

Swiss Darning (Duplicate Stitch)

Working horizontally or vertically, come out at base of stitch you want to cover, go under both legs of stitch above, then go back into base.

Fig. 100

Cross-Stitch on Stockinette

To cross a stockinette stitch, come up at lower-right corner of stitch (1), insert needle at upper-left corner (2), come up at lower-left corner (3), and cross over the knit stitch, inserting needle at upper-right corner (4).

BOBBIN BASICS

Untangling yarn bobbins

When you knit with different-color yarns on bobbins, they often get tangled. Here's a way to avoid the problem: After winding the yarn on a bobbin, slip a piece of a drinking straw over the end of the yarn so the yarn is drawn through the straw while you're knitting.

— *Mrs. M. Harrison, West Vancouver, BC, Canada*

No knitting-bobbin tangle

When using as many as 10 bobbins in a row for intarsia, I could never keep the bobbins straight and unsnarled as I went to turn my work. Now I place my needle along the top edge of a freestanding knitting basket, with the completed row face down and the bobbins hanging into the basket. Now it's easy to turn the basket and pick up the needle to do the next row, and the bobbins are in order and untangled.

— *Mimi Nelson, Trotwood, OH*

Homemade yarn bobbins

Recently I started a project that called for about 20 large knitting bobbins. It was inconvenient to go shopping for them, and it would have been expensive, so I improvised by using a few old, warped plastic food-storage containers and lids. I drew a pattern (shown full size in *Fig. 101*), traced it onto the plastic, and cut the bobbins out. They turned out to be better in every way than commercial bobbins: nonbrittle, inexpensive, and satisfying!

— *Gloria Albert, Shaker Heights, OH*

Fig. 101

Fig. 102

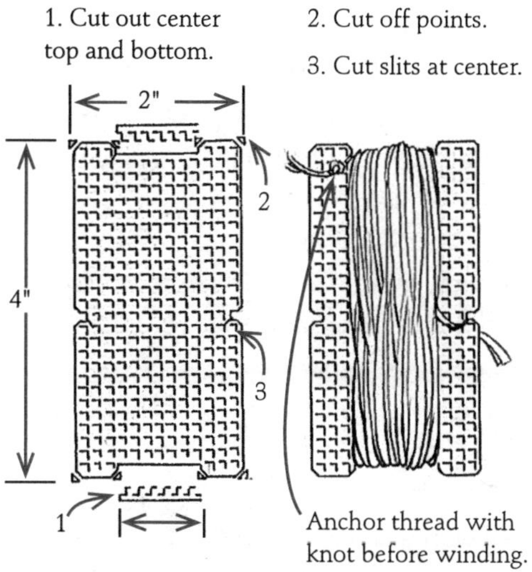

1. Cut out center top and bottom.

2. Cut off points.

3. Cut slits at center.

Anchor thread with knot before winding.

Low-cost, durable yarn bobbins

A good bobbin for weaving or knitting yarns is hard to find. I make my own from plastic needlepoint canvas, as shown in *Fig. 102*. I find the 2- by 4-inch size most useful, and anything larger than 4 inches not really firm enough to work with. After cutting, I smooth the plastic with an emery board.

— *Carol Hiebert, Downs, IL*

A slick bobbin for hand knitters

Machine knitters have a notion that I've never seen in a shop or catalog for hand knitters. It's a plastic yarn bobbin that snaps closed and greatly improves on traditional hand-wound bobbins for ease of winding and unwinding, protection of the yarn, and portability. The disc-shaped bobbin looks like a yo-yo, as shown in *Fig. 103*, but one side pops open to reveal the central core you wrap your yarn around. The side snaps shut to cover the yarn and secure the working end. You can easily unwind more yarn without opening the bobbin up. The bobbins come in three sizes, called Easy Bob (1⅞-inch diameter), Big Bob (3½ inches), and Giant Bob (6 inches), and all are inexpensive; 10 Easy Bobs are less than $3. These things are great for intarsia knitters and those who travel.

— *Hannelore Ring, San Diego, CA*

Fig. 103

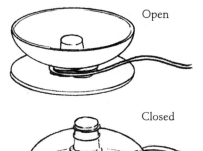

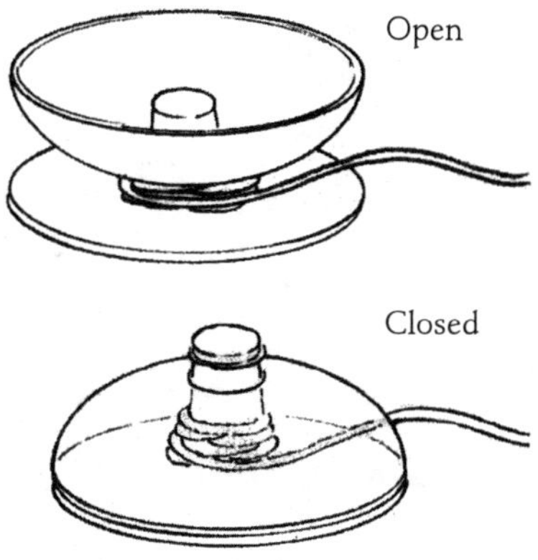

Open

Closed

Yarn butterflies

A yarn butterfly is useful whenever you need small lengths of yarn, such as for argyle knitting. The butterfly is a tiny center-pull skein that keeps the yarn out of your way when it's not in use. Place the yarn around your thumb so that the end dangles in your palm. Then wind as much yarn as you think you'll need in a figure eight between your thumb and little finger, as shown in the left drawing of *Fig. 104.* To secure the butterfly, tie the final end around the center of the bundle in two or three half hitches, as shown in the right drawing. Weave or knit from the end that dangled in your palm. If the butterfly loosens too much as you use the yarn, retie the half hitches.

Fig. 104

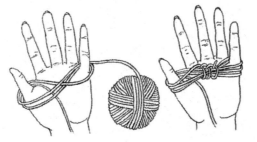

ODDS AND ENDS
Lefties are right on when knitting in two colors

I'm a lefty who's loved Continental knitting ever since I learned it. I retaught myself the right-handed throw so I could do stranded knitting effectively. But I prefer carrying the thread with my left hand. An antique ring on my left forefinger makes a convenient divider for two strands of colored yarn. I hold the more-often-used strand closer to the fingertip. When knitting in the round, I can easily pass the needle under the less-used thread to get the other if the carry is more than five stitches. So now I do stranding all Continental. I think it's easier for lefties to learn Continental, and do it just as the righties do.
— *Selma Miriam, Westport, CT*

Even gauge with color knitting

In knitting a two- or three-color pattern, I find that I get a much more even finished gauge if I use a needle one size larger on the multicolor rows than on the single-color rows that occur periodically in the design.
— *Betsy Carpenter, Los Altos, CA*

Fig. 105

A
F
E
D
C
B
A

Knitting up every scrap

I can't throw away any yarn or resist a wonderful ball on sale. This woven knitting technique using slipped stitches *(Fig. 105)* uses every scrap long enough to do a row. (See *Mary Thomas's Book of Knitting Patterns* under Hopsac Stitch or Barbara Walker's Tricolor Fabric Stitch in *A Treasury of Knitting Patterns*.) I change colors at the end of each row or every third row. The result is a dense bird's-eye-diaper-patterned fabric. The edges don't curl, and it can be cut and machine-stitched or combined with woven fabrics.

— *Bee Borssuck, Scottsdale, AZ*

Joining a new color

When working colorwork patterns, join new colors at the edge by tying a loop in the new yarn. Slip the old yarn through the loop, and pull the new yarn firmly up against the edge of the swatch *(Fig. 106)*. Then tie a square knot with the two ends. This may seem thick, but it prevents the ends from loosening, even if the yarns are slippery.

Fig. 106

Tie loop in new color; insert old color; pull tight.

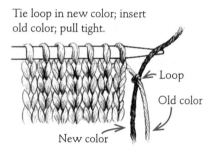

Loop

Old color

New color

FOUR

GARMENT-MAKING TIPS

Gauge

Patterns and Design

Cardigan Front Bands

Buttonholes and Buttons

Sleeves

Picking Up Stitches for Necklines
   and Armholes, and Shaping

Steeks, With and Without

Socks, Gloves, Hats, and Such

GAUGE

Successful swatching

Think about the swatch's size, shape, and edges before casting on. The most useful swatch measures at least 6 to 8 inches square. Generally speaking, the heavier the yarn, the larger the swatch should be to give you a feel for the finished fabric. Take an educated guess about your yarn and cast on enough stitches to yield 6 to 8 inches in width. For a worsted yarn yielding 5 stitches per inch, for example, I cast on 30 to 40 stitches. If I'm knitting a pattern that repeats, I cast on an even multiple within this stitch range.

I always add a garter or stockinette stitch or two to both sides of the swatch to help isolate the pattern and keep the swatch edges flat. Doing this also makes it easier to pick up stitches along the edge and seam the swatch if it is later used in the garment.

Starting or ending your swatch with ribbing or another edging will give you an idea of how these finishes will look on the sweater. To check the look of a cardigan front band, pick up stitches and knit a band along a side edge.

Finally, you can use your swatch to test finishing and blocking techniques. For example, I steam pure wool or mohair swatches to full the fibers slightly and stabilize the fabric. And I stretch or pull swatches made of stretchy yarns like rayon to simulate wear before measuring gauge.

— *Deborah Newton*

Determining gauge when designing your own patterns

When I design a sweater in a new yarn, I first check to see if the manufacturer has suggested a gauge for that yarn. I may not use that gauge in the final project, but if there is one given, I start my swatch-making in stockinette stitch with the recommended needles to get the stitch and row count that the manufacturer thinks makes a suitable fabric for the yarn. In my experience, manufacturers tend to suggest needles that are a little too large and a gauge that is a little too coarse, producing drapier fabrics than I like. But if you're the designer, the stiffness or drapiness of your knit fabric is entirely up to you. If you want to knit a lacy fabric, you might use needles four or five (or more) sizes larger than those recommended.

If your goal is a water-resistant gansey sweater, you're likely to use needles two or three sizes smaller. Either way, you'll want to experiment with needle sizes and stitch patterns until you produce a fabric that pleases you. That fabric will be the perfect gauge for your design.

Make your swatches about 6 inches square, so you can really test your results. Play with each swatch: Drape it over your bust or hips to see if it follows your shape or holds its own; feel it with your face to test it texture; hold it up to the light and breathe through it to test how light- and windproof it is. It's especially useful to compare your swatches with the fabric of sweaters you know and love. Every yarn offers many different possibilities for texture and drape. There isn't a single right answer.

Always knit your swatches in the pattern stitch you plan to use. If you plan to combine open and solid stitches, you'll need to find a compromise gauge that knits well in all your patterns, which can sometimes be a challenge.

If you're using a variety of yarns, you need to find a gauge that's in the middle range to suit the finest to the heaviest of the yarns. Knit your swatch on a needle that's too big for the fine yarn and too small for the thick ones. If it's drapey enough for the thick yarns but too flabby for the fine ones, try a slightly smaller needle. If it's fine with the thin yarns but produces a board with the heavy yarns, try using a somewhat thicker needle. If your range of yarns is extremely wide, you may never find a good compromise. To get something with a more consistent hang and drape, combine thinner yarns to produce a new yarn in the average weight range. You can combine all the different fiber types in a single garment if you're careful about cleaning; it may be necessary to dry-clean a complex fabric.

— *Alice Korach*

Calculating stitches

To calculate how many stitches you'll need for a given section of a sweater, start by measuring your gauge swatch to learn the stitch and row gauge. Measure and mark an area 4 inches wide and 4 inches long, preferably at the center. Count the number of stitches (horizontally) and rows (vertically) in this area, and divide by 4. This yields the number of stitches or rows you have per inch.

To calculate how many stitches and rows you'll need for a section of knitting, multiply your gauge (stitches/inch and rows/inch) by the width and length of the sweater section. For example, if the section measures 20 inches wide and your stitch gauge is 5 stitches/inch, then 20 inches x 5 stitches/inch = 100 stitches. If your section measures 10 inches long and your row gauge is 7 stitches per inch, then 10 inches x 7 rows/inch = 70 rows. So casting on 100 stitches and knitting for 70 rows will result in a section that's 20 inches wide and 10 inches long.

PATTERNS AND DESIGN
Making sweater "muslins"

Before starting a sweater in a pattern I've never made, I make a "muslin," or test garment, in inexpensive knit yardage. I use the measurements given in the pattern to make a paper pattern, then serge an inexpensive model of the garment to check the size and drape. Then, armed with my gauge swatch and the model sweater, I can easily adjust the pattern before casting on a single stitch.

— *Nan D. Carlson, Newark, NY*

Knitwear design with the aid of a photocopier

For an inexpensive knitwear design tool, I draw a basic drop-shoulder sweater shape on a sheet of paper, then photocopy it onto 8½- by 11-inch overhead transparency film using the copier's bypass/hand-feed option. (Transparency film for copiers is available at stationery stores and photocopy shops.) I then lay transparencies over interesting fabrics, prints, and textures to look for design inspirations. The transparencies go with me to fabric stores, flea markets, gardens, or museums—anyplace where ideas are likely to present themselves. I also make lots of plain white paper copies and use a large collection of colored markers to play with color ideas and details before beginning the final graphing process.

— *Jana Trent, Colleyville, TX*

Knitting for kids

There are many ways to build flexibility of size and appearance into a child's sweater. While it is important to design a sweater that will fit one child for several years, it is also wise to think of ways to make it suitable for others.

Designing for growth: The most obvious way to handle growth is to make the garment expandable. Wrists and belly buttons are often visible long before a child outgrows a sweater sideways. Make your ribbing extra long at the waist and wrist; a flat, inconspicuous seam, like mattress stitch, or circular knitting, which has no seams, will enable you to turn cuffs up in the beginning and down later. If the child is available for frequent fittings, a "top-down" design is a good idea, as it will allow you to unravel and reknit a longer waist and wrist later.

Another way of dealing with growth is to make the item versatile as a hand-me-down. Changing buttons can help considerably to make a sweater seem new again, as can the addition of embroideries.

You can do a lot to change the appearance of a garment by removing, adding, or altering edgings and borders.

Withstanding hard play: Children are tough on their outerwear, which handknits tend to be. They also get so involved in activities that they are careless of what is happening to their clothes. They will snatch off a mitten to pick up something and take off a cardigan when a game gets heated. Thus, your designs should take potential loss and damage into account.

Consider giving mittens in sets of three—or even five! Attaching them to strings for threading through coat sleeves is an option, but it's frequently resisted. An interesting alternative is to make sleeve cuffs into mittens that can be turned back when not in use. Cuff mittens are easiest to work round from the top down. Continue the cuff to the base of the thumb. For larger sizes, you'll probably want to add a few stitches for a thumb gusset. Put the thumb stitches on a holder and continue knitting until you reach the fingertips. Bind off half the stitches and work the other half back and forth to form a flap 2 or 3 inches long. Fold it back on itself so both sides of the mitten are the same

Measurements for Children's Sweaters (in Inches)

Age	6 mos	10 mos	2 yrs	3 yrs	4 yrs	5 yrs	6 yrs	7 yrs	8 yrs	9 yrs	10 yrs
Chest	to 20	to 22	21	22	23	24	25	26	27	28.5	30
Waist	19	20	20	20.5	21	21.5	22	22.5	23	24	25
Hip	20	21	22	23	24	25	26	27	28	30	32
Back-waist length	7	7.5	8.5	9	9.5	10	10.5	11.5	12.5	14	15
Across back	7.75	8.25	8.75	9.25	9.5	9.75	10.25	10.75	11	11.5	12
Shoulder	2.25	2.5	2.75	3	3	3	3.5	3.5	3.5	3.75	4
Back neck	3.25	3.25	3.25	3.25	3.5	3.5	3.5	3.75	3.75	4	4
Underarm sleeve	6.5	7.5	8.5	9.5	10.5	11	11.5	12	12.5	13.5	15
Armhole depth	3.5	3.75	4.25	4.75	5.5	5.5	6	6	6.25	6.5	7
Upper-arm width	7	7.25	7.5	7.75	8	8.25	8.5	8.75	9	9.5	9.75
Wrist width	5	5	5.25	5.25	5.5	5.5	5.5	5.75	5.75	6	6
Head	15	16	17	18	18	18	18	18	18	18	18

length and stitch the edges to the sides of the hand. Fold the flap over the fingertips to close the mitten. You can sew Velcro® strips on the flap, hand, and cuff for extra security. To complete the thumb, work the stitches on the holder, picking up others as needed.

Potential damage can be minimized if you design for easy repair, particularly if you knit the garment from the neck down to make the vulnerable cuffs and elbows easy to replace. You can reinforce elbows by adding knit or woven material patches or cross-stitch embroidery or, more interestingly, by working a doubled yarn stripe or woven color pattern at elbow length. A slip-stitch pattern is good, too, because it produces a double-knit fabric.

— *Judith Eckhardt Greer*

CARDIGAN FRONT BANDS
Rib as you go

If you're making a cardigan, you'll find it easier to knit the ribbing for the front edges while you knit the body of the sweater. You'll eliminate the need to sew the ribbing later, and you'll also be assured of a row-for-row match. However, you must change to needles that are smaller than those you're using on the body so the ribbing won't sag. Use a pair of double-pointed needles one or two sizes smaller than those on which you are knitting the body. Knit the ribbing stitches with the smaller needles. Then continue across the work with the regular needles. Turn the work around, work across

the row, and, when you get to the ribbing, pick up the double-pointed needles to work the ribbing stitches. Your ribbing will be the perfect length.

Taking the turn out of cardigan front bands

Plain vertical edges of stockinette stitch will roll if no edging is added, since it is the nature of the stockinette fabric to roll to the purl side. Thus, some sort of band must be provided at the front closing of a cardigan. A fold-under band in stockinette solves the problem, but the doubled fabric adds extra weight, and so these bands tend to sag. A band of knit one, purl one vertical ribbing is never advised, since all ribbing stretches lengthwise, and, in time, this band will cause the front of the sweater to grow longer.

There are three preferred solutions for cardigan front bands. The first is to knit them in garter stitch, at least seven stitches wide. Garter stitch is elastic lengthwise and makes attractive one-row buttonholes.

The second solution is to knit them in seed stitch, again making them at least seven stitches wide. Three-row buttonholes are good-looking in this band. With either type of band, do not make a vertical line of purl stitches on the outside of the knitted piece separating the garment from the band, as these will form a fold line, which will cause the band to turn forward.

The third solution is to make single-crochet bands after completing the rest of the garment. Working each row the length of the band, crochet the final row, including the bottom and top edges, in crab stitch (single crochet worked left to right instead of right to left). The corners of the crochet bands tend to curl and will need occasional steaming to lie flat.

After you complete your cardigan sweater, hand-wash and block it or have it dry-cleaned if it is not washable. Then either send the garment out to be steam-blocked or steam-block it yourself if you feel competent to do so, being exceedingly careful not to stretch the hot, damp fabric. The loving touch of hot steam on a clean garment will set the bands in the position you want them.

— *Maggie Righetti*

A ribbing band knit along with a sweater

Knitting the ribbing band of a cardigan at the same time as the body is a great idea. Unfortunately, ribbing stretches more than stockinette stitch and will sag if it is knit at the same gauge, but who wants to change gauge midrow?

Here's what I do. About every 3 or 4 inches, I knit a short row on the body of the sweater: I knit across the body of the sweater up to the ribbing, turn, slip the first stitch, and continue back across the body. On the next row, I continue all the way across the ribbing. This keeps the ribbing shorter and eliminates sagging.

— *Jean Dickinson, Williamstown, VT*

Knitting two pieces at once

I prefer to knit both cardigan sweater fronts at the same time. To keep the two balls of yarn from tangling, I put each in a soup bowl on the floor.

— *Ann Ingraham, Eureka, CA*

Cardigan buttonhole band

I've never liked any predesigned buttonhole band, so I designed one that works in one step, which not only looks nice on any pattern, but lies flat and is complete as is. It is worked across five stitches, but can be extended to seven or nine stitches to give a final width of approximately 1 inch.

Right side:
K1, k1, p1, k1, k1.

Wrong side:
K1, p1, k1, p1, k1.

Buttonhole (worked on right side):
K1, k1, yo, k2tog, k1.

This gives the final effect of a knit one, purl one ribbed band, but without the disadvantage of the natural pulling-in of ribbing. The seed-stitch edging (one stitch each edge of band) keeps it flat. The only trick is in pulling the yarn tightly to knit the outside finished edge. When the sweater is complete, this band doesn't stretch or need stretching via blocking, as it's worked in parallel with the sweater.

— *Mary R. Studeny, New Rochelle, NY*

90

BUTTONHOLES AND BUTTONS
Pick your buttonhole

Practice these buttonholes by casting on 20 stitches in sport- or medium-weight yarn using needles two sizes smaller than for the body of the work, and working knit one, purl one rib for about 1 inch. Mark the right side of your swatch and work all the buttonholes from this side.

Eyelet buttonhole: Eyelets are good for small buttons and look neat on a knit one, purl one ribbed band or in the purl ribs of knit two, purl two ribbing. They're unobtrusive but not very tailored looking on stockinette.

For a small eyelet (1 row), work k1, p1 for 9 sts, ending k1 (buttonhole will be in purl trough). Yarn to the front (makes an automatic yo), k2tog. Finish p1, k1 to end. A large eyelet takes 3 rows:

Row 1:
Work k1, p1 for 9 sts, ending k1. Yo twice. K2tog, p1, k1 to end of row.

Row 2:
Rib to yo's, ending p1. Knit first yo, drop second yo, p1, k1 to end of row.

Row 3:

Rib to buttonhole and purl into hole below. Complete row.

Vertical slit (even number of rows): Good for any size button. The chain selvages along the slit roll to the back, making it blend perfectly into the ribbing. When working this buttonhole in stockinette, don't work the increase, which is there only to align the knit ribs.

Row 1:

Work k1, p1 for 10 sts, ending p1. *With a separate strand of yarn,* purl into st below next st (inc 1 st), k1, p1 to end of row.

Row 2:

K1, p1 to buttonhole, ending k1 in inc st. Pick up original strand of yarn, insert right needle knitwise into first st, pull yarn gently, and slip st to right needle. P1, k1 to end of row.

Row 3:

K1, p1 to buttonhole, ending p1. With second strand of yarn and yarn in front, slip first st purlwise, pulling gently on yarn. K1, p1 to end of row.

Rows 4 and 5:

Repeat Rows 2 and 3 as many times as needed.

Row 6:

K1, p1 to within 1 st of opening. To close buttonhole from WS, k2tog at top of slit. Rib to end of row. Cut separate strand and darn in ends.

Self-reinforcing buttonhole, horizontal (1 row): This can lie horizontally or vertically. Worked over an odd number of stitches on a knit one, purl one ribbed border, it will fall neatly between purl troughs. It also looks neat worked from the wrong side.

Step 1:

K1, p1 for 8 sts, ending p1.

Step 2:

Slip next st purlwise.

Step 3:

Pass first slipped st over second (1 st bound off). Slipping sts from the left to the right needle, continue binding off for a total of 5 sts.

Step 4:

Slip last bound-off st from right to left needle. Turn work.

Step 5:

With yarn in back, cast on 6 sts (1 st more than bound off) using cable cast-on as

Three-Row Buttonhole

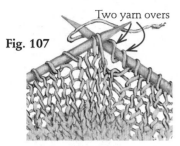

Fig. 107

Two yarn overs

First buttonhole row:
Knit two together through
backs of stitches.

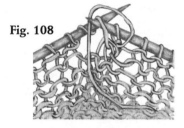

Fig. 108

Second buttonhole row:
Purl first yarn over, then
drop second yarn over.

Two yarn overs

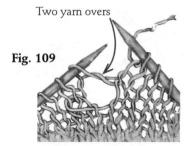

Fig. 109

Third buttonhole row:
Knit into the hole below
the next stitch.

follows: Insert right needle between first and second sts on left needle, and draw through a loop. Slip loop onto left needle (first cast-on st). Repeat, inserting right needle between last cast-on st and previous st. Before putting the last cast-on st onto left needle, bring yarn to front. Turn work.

Step 6:
Slip first st from left to right needle and pass last cast-on st over it. Rib to end of row.
— *Pam Allen*

Two styles of buttonholes

Three-row buttonhole: The three-row buttonhole is a hand knitter's dream. It works in any pattern stitch, needs no final finishing, and is easy to remember and make. It is a vertical buttonhole that's three rows high. The size varies according to the yarn and needles used, but the button size appropriate for the yarn will usually fit the hole.

First row:
On the right side of the work, work to desired location of the buttonhole, yarn over twice, knit the next two stitches together by knitting into the backs of the stitches, and continue across the row *(Fig. 107)*.

Second row:
On the wrong side of the work, work to the location of the buttonhole, purl one (first yarn over), drop the next stitch (second yarn over) off the needle, and continue across the row *(Fig. 108)*. I know it looks terrible, but have faith.

Third row:
On the right side of the work, work to the buttonhole, knit into the hole (below the next stitch), drop the next stitch, then continue across the row *(Fig. 109)*. Now continue to work in pattern stitch.

One-row buttonhole: The one-row buttonhole can be made any size you want. It is more complicated to knit and harder to remember, but it creates a nice horizontal opening. With the right side of the work facing you, work in pattern stitch to the desired location. Slip the next stitch knitwise (as if to knit) onto the right needle. Bring the yarn between the tips of the needles to the front of the work and drop it *(Fig. 110)*. Without knitting any stitches, bind off the number of stitches needed to make the size buttonhole you want. Binding off four stitches, for example, will give you a buttonhole that's four stitches wide. To bind off, slip the next stitch onto the right needle purlwise (as if to purl) and, with the tip of the left needle, lift the first slipped stitch up and over the second and off the needle. Then slip the next stitch knitwise from the left needle to the right and lift the previously slipped stitch up, over, and off the needle (*Fig. 111*). (Slipping the stitches first purlwise and then knitwise keeps the buttonhole's bottom edge from curling out.) Continue until the hole is as long as you want it.

Move the last stitch on the right needle to the left needle. Turn the work around so the wrong side is facing you. Bring the yarn that's now at the back of the work between the needles to the front and cast on purlwise one more stitch than you bound off, as follows: Insert the right needle into the front of the first stitch on the left needle and make a purl stitch, but don't take the old stitch off the left needle. Move the new stitch to the left needle by inserting it into the front of the new stitch from right to left (*Fig. 112*).

When the necessary stitches are cast on, turn the work around again so you are working in the original direction (right side of work facing you). Move the first stitch on the right needle to the left needle. Knit two

together. Continue across the row. Then work another row or two to appreciate the good looks of the one-row buttonhole.

—*Maggie Righetti*

Knit buttonholes you won't mind seeing

I like to hand-sew around the buttonholes in my handknits. If I'm using a three- or four-ply yarn, I separate the plies and use one or two plies to do buttonhole stitch around the buttonhole. This makes a really neat buttonhole, which I whip shut until the sweater is blocked. I also use one or two plies to sew the button on.

—*Elizabeth Custer, Creston, IA*

Perfect placement for knit buttonholes

In published sweater patterns, horizontal buttonholes are invariably placed dead center on the buttonhole band. If you sew the button in the center of the button band, the closed garment will reveal the inner edge of the button band because the buttonholes are always under stress when the buttons are

One-Row Buttonhole

Fig. 110

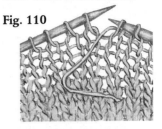

Slip next stitch knitwise and bring yarn to front of work.

Fig. 111

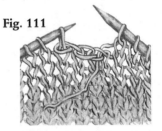

Bind off required number of stitches and move last slipped stitch to left needle.

Fig. 112

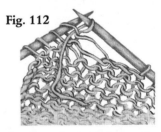

Cast on purlwise, make a purl stitch, but don't take stitch off left needle. Then insert left needle in front of new stitch from right to left.

Fig. 113

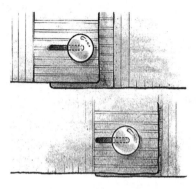

Gapping occurs when button and buttonhole are both centered. Cardigan closes perfectly when buttonhole edge is at center of band.

done up (top drawing of *Fig. 113*). The larger the button and buttonhole, the more the button band will show. Sewing the button toward the inside of the band allows the borders to lie correctly but makes the button appear off center.

To make the two borders lie properly aligned and the button appear in the center of the band, offset the buttonhole so its outer edge is the center stitch of the buttonhole band. Then sew the button in the center of

its band. The closed button will appear in the center of the border, and the borders will lie correctly (bottom drawing of *Fig. 113*).
—*The Right Reverend Richard Rutt, former Bishop of Leicester, Leicester, England*

Knit buttonholes for girls or boys

I knit a sweater with the buttonholes on both fronts for an as-yet-to-be-born baby. When the baby is born, the buttons can be sewn on the appropriate side, closing the hole beneath. If the sweater is passed on to another child or sibling of the opposite sex, the buttons can be transferred easily to the other side.
—*Marion E. Scoular, Duluth, GA*

Invisible buttonholes

Hiding a sweater's buttonholes in the purl part of a knit one, purl one rib can be very effective. This is the method I use. When I'm ready to knit the first buttonhole, I work half the rib stitches, ending on a knit stitch as seen from the front. Using a separate piece of yarn, I work the last half of the rib stitches and continue to work each side of the buttonhole with separate yarn until it's the right length. Then I drop the added strand and work all the way across the ribbing with the original skein. I carry the extra strand by twisting it loosely in the back when I'm ribbing from the right side. On the wrong side of the work, I ignore it.

I carry the strand up this way until I come to the next buttonhole. If the strand runs out, I work in another, as I did at the beginning. This is as invisible a knit buttonhole as I've ever seen.

—Alice Smock, Mercer Island, WA

Two crocheted buttons

You can crochet a small stuffed ball or you can cover a flat button. To get the right effect, play with the directions below, varying hook size and number of stitches and rounds.

Ball button: Using a crochet hook several sizes smaller than you'd ordinarily use with your yarn, ch 3. Join into ring with sl st, ch 1.

Round 1:
Work 6 sc into ring. Join with sl st, ch 1.

Round 2:
1 sc in next sc, 2 sc in next sc. Repeat from * to * around (9 sts). Join, ch 1.

Round 3:
Work 1 sc in each sc. Join, ch 1.

Round 4:
Decrease: *Insert hook into next sc, yo, draw loop through; insert hook into next sc, yo, and draw loop through; yo and draw loop through all 3 loops on hook*. Continue from * to *, working decreases until opening is almost closed.

Insert a wooden bead (10 mm is a good size) or stuff with yarn. Close opening with more spiral decreases if ball isn't covered, or thread yarn on a tapestry needle and run through remaining sc's to gather up. Cut yarn, pull tail through, and use it to sew on button.

Some yarns will require that you ch 2 for the initial ring, some ch 4. You may be able to fit more sc's in the initial ring, maybe fewer. You may not need the even round of sc's. Instead, you may need to dec on the round immediately following the inc round. If your yarn is too thick, and plied, you may want to work with just one ply. Cut a 5-foot length. Clip a clothespin on one end and separate the plies from the other end.

Flat button: Ch 3 and join into ring with sl st, ch 1.

Round 1:
Work 6 sc into ring, join with sl st, ch 1.

Round 2:
Work 2 sc in each sc (12 sc). Join, ch 1.

Round 3:
Decrease: Inserting hook into back loops of sc stitches, *insert hook into first sc, yo, and draw loop through; insert hook into next sc, yo, and draw loop through; yo and draw loop through all 3 loops on hook*. Continue from * to *, inserting a flat button the same color as the yarn after the first round. Work decreases until entire button is covered. Cut yarn, pull tail through, and use it to sew on button. Improvise however you wish.

— *Pam Allen*

Making dorset buttons

Dorset buttons provide a beautiful finishing touch for special knitted, crocheted, or sewn garments. They are made by embroidering a single length of thread over and around a suitably sized ring. You can use any type of thread, from fine embroidery silk to knitting yarn. For the ring, choose smooth metal, bone, or plastic in the desired size.

Use a blunt tapestry needle for working the button, but change to a sharp one for finishing if you prefer. You must begin with a very long thread as you cannot join more thread until you start covering the spokes. Tie the thread to the ring, hold the loose end behind the ring, and work the first six or seven buttonhole stitches over it. Cut off any excess thread tail.

Cover the ring with buttonhole stitches, as shown in *Fig. 114,* keeping them tight and close together so the ring doesn't show through. Slip your needle through the first stitch so the join is invisible.

Turn all stitches inward so the outside of the ring is smooth and the ridge is on the inside.

With the thread at the back of the ring, lay the spokes of the button by bringing the thread down to the bottom of the ring, then up in front at the exact center. Rotate the ring an eighth turn and wind again from back to front. Continue until you have made eight spokes. Fasten these securely by making a cross in the middle: bring the needle up where the first spoke was made and over the last, and repeat from side to side, keeping the cross exactly in the center of the ring. (The front and back threads will not align until you make the center cross. Don't be alarmed by this.)

To fill, or round, the button, backstitch over each of the spokes, keeping the thread taut and even. Fill in as much as you like, leaving a long thread to sew the button to the garment. You can make a shank for sewing on the button, using a knitting needle as a gauge. If you prefer to round the button using a different color, change threads by working over the new thread at the back for a few stitches, picking up the new color and working over the old for a few stitches. Clip the thread ends.

By arranging the spokes differently, you can make a variety of designs. Thanks to *SlipKnot*, the official magazine of The Knitting and Crochet Guild of Great Britain, for permission to reprint this tip from their issue No. 47.

— *Lesley Conroy, Bradford, England*

Fig. 114

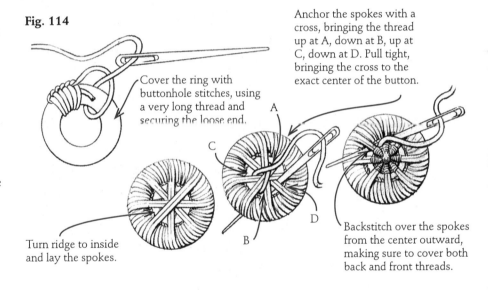

Cover the ring with buttonhole stitches, using a very long thread and securing the loose end.

Turn ridge to inside and lay the spokes.

Anchor the spokes with a cross, bringing the thread up at A, down at B, up at C, down at D. Pull tight, bringing the cross to the exact center of the button.

Backstitch over the spokes from the center outward, making sure to cover both back and front threads.

SLEEVES

Even sleeves

I always knit the two fronts of a cardigan or two sleeves at the same time from two balls of yarn. To make sure I knit the same number of rows on each piece, I have to remember not to lay the knitting down with one front or sleeve on each needle. I do this by pinning the pieces together with coilless safety pins about every two inches as the work progresses. This makes it look more like one piece and helps avoid mistakes.

— *Charlotte Stafford, Chesterland, OH*

Knitting from both ends

I like to knit both sleeves at the same time. I knit from both ends of the same ball, one end for each sleeve. This is especially useful for mittens and socks, when you want equal stripes in the pair and you want to use up odd bits of yarn.

— *Betsy Carpenter, Los Altos, CA*

Knitting sleeves from the top down

I usually knit on a circular needle and pick up and knit the sleeves from the shoulder down. To avoid the fuzziness that can occur from overhandling knit garments, particularly on softer yarns like merino, I fold the sweater neatly and place it in a plastic bag (not cloth), leaving the picked-up shoulder stitches available at the opening of the bag. To further secure the bag, you can tie a string around the outside.

— *Barbara Bononno, New York, NY*

Knitted sleeves that match

For even sleeves with fewer mistakes, start by working both sleeves on the same needle until the ribbing is completed. Then either work to the first increase or to the end of the first pattern. At this point, begin to knit each sleeve separately, measuring length by rows, patterned rows, or increases. At the armhole decreases, begin working the sleeves together again until finished.

— *Mary Papageorgiou, Madison, CT*

Knitting sleeves before the body

Knit your sleeves first, not last. That way you can correct a gauge or pattern problem with fewer stitches to rip out. Also, you are guaranteeing that you will end up with a sweater, and not just another vest, as I often have if I get bored after knitting just the body.

— *Beth A. Kollé, Seattle, WA*

Tapered ribbing for cuffs

I use tapered ribbing on cuffs that are meant to lie flat. I usually work sleeves from the shoulders down, but if you're working from the bottom up, you can use an invisible cast-on for the sleeves and work the cuff last.

Pick up stitches for the cuff rib, gathering for size, if necessary, in the first row. Knit about two-thirds of the length of the cuff on the size needles you chose for the ribbing. Then change to one size smaller and knit one row. Alternate knitting one row with the ribbing needles and one with the smaller needles a few times to produce a smooth transition. Then rib to the row before the last with the smaller needles. Rib the last row on the ribbing needles; insert the smaller needles—without knitting—and bind off with a tubular method. When using worsted- or bulky-weight yarn, I begin the taper about one-third of the way down a 3-inch cuff and change successively to needles two sizes smaller.

— *Patricia Tongue Edraos, Boston, MA*

Decreasing for sleeve cuffs

On a child's sweater, I like to eliminate 1½ to 2 inches' worth of stitches when I get to the cuff (knitting down from the shoulder), and on an adult's sweater, I eliminate up to 3 inches. Often when I say this, people worry that the sleeve will have a puffy look, but it doesn't. This much of a decrease gives you a comfortable sleeve that doesn't pull or drag when worn over a long-sleeved shirt.

— *Jean Baker White, North Haven, ME*

Easy sweater armhole facing

When I knit sleeves in the round for a drop-shoulder sweater, I add an inch to the sweater's sleeve length. When I set the sleeve into the body and sew it, I use the extra inch to cover and bind the cut edge on the body.
— *Beth A. Kollé, Seattle, WA*

Setting in knitted sleeves

Knitters often spoil sweaters when setting in sleeves. For professional-looking set-in sleeves, I use a dressmaking technique: Hold the garment and sleeve at the shoulder seam, right sides together, cupping the sleeve cap over your curved fingers and keeping the two edges together with your thumb *(Fig. 115)*. Pin closely. Then backstitch, still cupping the cap. To get it perfectly rounded, I ignore the shape of the knit edges. Excess fabric adds welcome bulk under the shoulder, and the cupping distributes the extra fullness evenly. If the cap is too wide to work in evenly,

Fig. 115

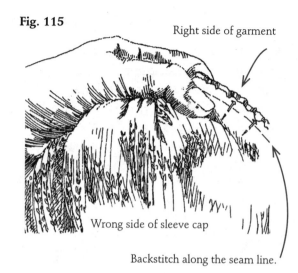

Right side of garment

Wrong side of sleeve cap

Backstitch along the seam line.

before I sew the sleeve to the shoulder seam I run a piece of yarn through the top of the sleeve to gather it, and sometimes I crochet the edge to firm it.
— *Marne Chandler, Portola Valley, CA*

Drop-shoulder sleeve seams

My method of inserting drop-shoulder sleeves into the armhole makes a flat, clean, professional-looking seam on all yarns, even bulky cottons. Knit front shoulder seams to back shoulder seams. When the sleeve—knit from the wrist up—is finished, do not bind off. Instead, knit three or four rows of stockinette in a contrasting color of the same weight, using scrap yarn. Lay the body of the sweater out flat, right side up. Line up the center of the sleeve, right side down, over the shoulder seam with the edge of the sleeve even with the body selvage and the scrap knitting extending beyond the armhole (*Fig. 116*). Pin in place.

Insert a crochet hook, equal to the knitting-needle size, from the top through the first raw sleeve stitch—avoid the scrap yarn that goes into the stitch—and through the selvage stitch on the body edge. With a long length of sweater yarn, pull up a loop through the body selvage and sleeve—one loop on the hook. Insert the hook through the next raw sleeve stitch and body selvage, and draw up another loop—two loops on the hook. Pull the second stitch through first. Continue across the sleeve top, being sure to insert the hook through the raw sleeve stitches so you don't drop any. Unravel and discard the contrast yarn.

— *Karen Hoyle, Excelsior, MN*

Binding in a set-in sleeve

To attach set-in sleeves. I pin the sleeve to the armhole edge, right sides together, after joining the shoulder seam. Then, from the wrong side using a size 2 needle, I pick up and knit one stitch, then another through both layers at once, just inside the selvages. I bind the first stitch off over the second and continue in this manner around the armhole, as shown in *Fig. 117*. The result is a knitted seam that makes the two edges blend smoothly on the right side.

— *Laura Jones, Greer, SC*

Fig. 117

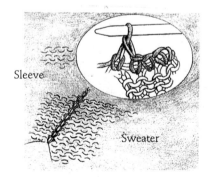

With sleeve and armhole right sides together, pick up and knit a stitch, then another, then bind off the first to set in a sleeve almost invisibly.

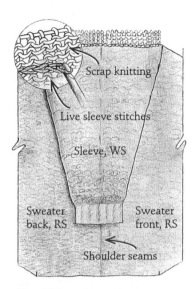

Fig. 116

After joining front to back at shoulders, center sleeve on shoulder, right sides together, with scrap knitting extending past the body selvage. Slip-stitch crochet all live sleeve stitches to body selvage.

Fig. 118

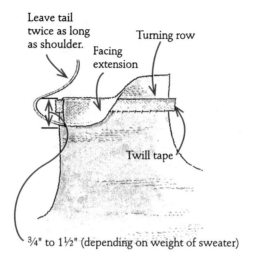

Leave tail twice as long as shoulder.

Facing extension

Turning row

Twill tape

¾" to 1½" (depending on weight of sweater)

Prevent stretched sweater shoulders

Oversized sweaters knit with natural fibers often stretch over the shoulders. A handy technique for preventing stretch is to add facing extensions to support the shoulders. I knit the shoulder on both front and back as instructed. When I reach the bind-off row, I knit a turning row of purl. If I'm not working in stockinette, I knit a definite line by ceasing the pattern stitch and working a plain stitch that I can see. After the turning row, I continue knitting in stockinette *(Fig. 118)*.

For added stability and absolutely no stretch, hand-stitch twill tape along the turning row with sewing thread. Sew the facing in place with the yarn tail. Graft the front and back together along the turning rows for an obvious seam, and in the valleys next to the rows for an invisible one. These facings will support the shoulders so they don't creep downward.

— *Shelly Cypher Springer,*
San Clemente, CA

PICKING UP STITCHES FOR NECKLINES AND ARMHOLES, AND SHAPING

How to pick up and knit

Picking up and knitting the stitches for a neck or an armhole ribbing is an all-in-one process. Working from the right side of the garment, unless directed otherwise, insert the right needle into a stitch at the right corner edge of the piece. Using the needle's point, pick up the yarn for the ribbing from behind the piece, just as if you were knitting the stitch, and pull it through the stitch to the front. Thus, one rib stitch has been picked up and knitted onto the needle. Continue to pick up and knit the ribbing stitches across the edge of the piece, working from right to left. When you're finished, you've knitted the first row of ribbing. Turn the work and continue in your ribbing stitch. If you're a left-handed knitter, work in the same way, but use the left needle for picking up stitches and work them from left to right.

If you are working with a fine yarn, you might find it easier to pick up the stitches with an appropriate size crochet hook. Then slip the loop onto the right needle. Remember to work from right to left.

— *Charlotte Biro*

Ribbing on single-pointed needles

Despite all the interest in circular needles and round knitting these days, I still like to use two needles and knit back and forth. Here's my method for knitting ribbing around armholes and necklines with single-pointed needles.

After front and back are complete, I sew one shoulder seam. Starting at one side-seam end of that armhole, I divide the armhole into four sections, two on each side of the shoulder seam. This simplifies distributing the required number of stitches evenly across it. I pick up the stitches and knit on the ribbing I want, then bind off and sew up that side seam, along with the ribbing.

Dividing the neckline in the same way, I pick up the stitches I need, starting at one side of the open shoulder and ending on the other side. I work the ribbing back and forth, bind off, and sew the shoulder and neckband together. I pick up the stitches on the second armhole the same way as on the first. Then I sew that side seam and ribbing together.

— *Genevieve Smolik, Parma Heights, OH*

Picking up neckline stitches with a crochet hook

When picking up stitches around necklines, especially with fuzzy yarns, I hold the yarn at the back of the work and pick up the stitches with a crochet hook; I put the hook through the stitch at the front, draw the thread through, and place the stitches on a circular needle. This method is very fast and always picks up the correct number of stitches.

— *Freda Jarjoura, Gatineau, PQ, Canada*

Neat knit neckband

For an easy-to-knit neckband that can be bound off and sewn down in one step, try the following method. It works best on a crew neck worked on circular needles, but it can also be used for cardigan bands knit horizontally.

Complete the band, keeping all stitches on the needle. Turn the neckband to the inside just as you would to sew it down. (A quick way to make the turn easy is to knit one row of purl stitches where the neckband is to be folded to the inside.) Insert the right needle into the first stitch, then into the corresponding purl bump at the start of the neckband where stitches were first picked up, as shown in *Fig. 119*. (I find it easier to put five or six of these sweater purl stitches back on a smaller double-pointed needle so I can easily find them.) Knit these two stitches together. *Knit the next stitch and purl bump together. Bind off the first stitch on the right needle by slipping it over the second stitch. Repeat from * around the neckband. Work loosely to give enough ease for the sweater to slip easily over the head.

— *Diane Zangl, Lomira, WI*

Fig. 119

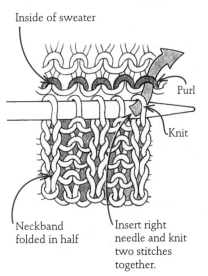

Inside of sweater

Purl

Knit

Neckband folded in half

Insert right needle and knit two stitches together.

Neat neck-edge pick-up

To avoid a loose first stitch when picking up along a neck edge, pick up the first stitch as usual, but pick up the second stitch by working a yarn over with both the working yarn and the tail. Besides securing the loose tail, this method also helps you keep tension on the first stitch. Pick up the other stitches as usual. On the next row, work the stitch with two loops as one.

— *Kathe Brinkmann, Urbana, IL*

Crochet an even knit selvage

Because I knit many fibers and colors into my garments, neck and shoulder selvages are irregular. Before picking up stitches for collars, sleeves, and finishes, I work a row of single crochet into the knit edges, creating an even selvage. I use a firm, medium-tone yarn. Picking up stitches between the single crochet and knit edge is easy, and the new section drapes well.

— *Claire Marcus, Newfoundland, PA*

Picking up knitting on fabric

My method for picking up knitting stitches along a fabric edge produces a very smooth, even join without pulling the knitting through the fabric. I also use it when I need to pick up stitches along the edge of a knit garment that has been worked with an irregular yarn, such as bouclé or other loopy or bulky fibers.

To join knitting to fabric, embroider a row of even chain stitches along the seamline of the fabric piece. With your knitting needle, pick up a stitch beneath both threads of each

chain stitch, as shown in *Fig. 120,* without going through the fabric. In addition to producing evenly spaced knit stitches, this will fold the seam allowance back to the wrong side. To join knitting to knitting, work the chain stitches close to the edge of the knit piece. This works particularly well when you need a perfect binding for a convex or concave shape.

— *Ilse Altherr, Lancaster, NH*

Fig. 120

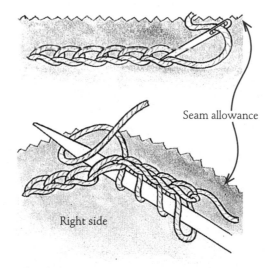

Seam allowance

Right side

Embroider a chain stitch along the seam allowance. Insert a knitting needle through both loops of the chain, pulling a knit stitch through.

Planning neck and shoulder shaping

Whether a sweater is knit in strips or in back and front pieces, you need to lower and curve the back and front necklines to allow for body contours and good fit. A straight back neck bound off even with the top of the shoulders often lies in a lump of fabric at the base of the collar—particularly if the fabric is heavy. I plot neck and shoulder shaping row for row and stitch for stitch on graph paper. You'll find this particularly helpful with a strip garment since the shaping will involve several strips at different places. A medium-size back neck is generally 7 to 8 inches wide (as is the front, but deeper). But each garment may be a little different. Measure the back neck of a sweater that fits and has a similar weight fabric.

Calculate the number of stitches you'll need for your neck width. The rest of the back stitches are divided evenly between the two shoulders. The front shoulders will have exactly the same number of stitches as the back, and for a symmetrical garment, the same number of stitches will compose both front and back necklines.

For a warm outerwear garment, like a coat, with a fairly high neckline, I would lower the center-front neckline only 2 inches, rather than the 2½ to 3 inches I would normally choose for a crewneck sweater. For a close fit at the back of the neck, I seldom lower it more than 1 inch. But a slight lowering and curve is important to fit the body's contours.

Back neck and shoulders: I usually bind off the middle half to three-quarters of the stitches all at once. From the point, you'll have to work each side of the neck curve separately. First, bind off two or three shallow stair steps. Each step is about 1 inch wide. When you've taken as many stitches out of the curve as you desire, work the edge straight until the piece is done.

Back shoulder shaping often begins at the same time or within two rows of back-neck shaping. Depending on shoulder width and the number of rows it takes to work 1 inch, I divide the stitches evenly into three or four groups and bind off that number at the beginning of each armhole edge. When I've bound off the last group, no back stitches remain.

Front neck and shoulders: Since the front neck begins lower than the back neck, the curve must be more gradual, so bind off a third to half the number of front-neck stitches. Work more and smaller bind-off steps along each side of the front neck than those on the back neck. Then decrease one stitch every other row on each neck edge until only the shoulder stitches remain. Work even until the front is just short of the four to six rows required for the shoulder shaping. Complete shoulder shaping just as for the back, being sure to begin each side at the armhole edge.

Neckline shaping for a pullover or cardigan: For a well-fitted neckline, use bind-off steps to shape the curve. The back curve is shallower than the front, but both have the same number of stitches. Shoulders are bound off in steps for a natural slope.

STEEKS, WITH AND WITHOUT

Steeks 101

To create openings for armholes or a front placket on a sweater knitted in the round, you can fill the spaces with steeks, then sew and cut them to open. To make a steek, first knit to where the base of the opening needs to be, and bind off about an inch of stitches, usually five or seven stitches. (You need an odd number of stitches so you'll have a center stitch for cutting.) The bound-off edge serves as a smooth base for later attaching a placket front or sleeve. On the next round, cast on the same number of stitches above the bound-off stitches, by simply twisting backward loops onto the right needle *(Fig. 121)*. On the following rounds, knit the steek stitches in alternating colors, creating vertical stripes so the cutting line will be easy to see. When you reach the top of the armhole or placket, bind off the steek stitches. Weave in all nearby ends, then baste down the center stitch of the steek in a contrasting color yarn.

Before cutting the steek, machine-sew with a medium-length stitch down the center of the stitch on each side of the basted stitch,

Fig. 121

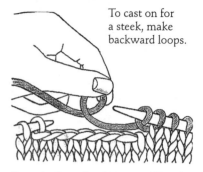

To cast on for a steek, make backward loops.

Bound-off stitches below steek

backstitching at top and bottom through bound-off and cast-on edges to secure. Carefully cut down the basted centerline. After you sew the sleeve into the opening or pick up stitches for a placket opening, tack the edges of the steek to the inside.

Improved steek cutting

Here's a simple solution to the problem of knit fabric stretching when you're machine-stitching along the sides of the steek on a cardigan sweater prior to cutting it. First, hand-baste with a contrasting thread up the center-front stitches. Then, turn the sweater inside out and fuse a strip of stabilizer about 2 inches wide up the center. Next, turn the sweater right-side out and cut along the basted line. Not only does the stabilizer keep the front from stretching, it also keeps the edges from raveling while you apply grosgrain ribbon to the front of the cardigan. You can tear off the stabilizer as you apply the ribbon.

— *Pamela Costello, Vadnais Heights, MN*

Sweaters in the round without steeks

I like to knit sweaters in the round, but I don't like to use steeks for sleeve openings, as it takes forever to weave the ends in when finishing. And I don't like to machine-stitch and then cut sleeve openings, because of the gaps and strained stitches where the armhole stops and the sweater begins.

So here's another way. When you reach the row where you want the sleeve opening to begin, knit in your pattern to two stitches before the point where the sleeve opening will begin. Place a marker, then increase about 1 inch of new stitches over the next four stitches and place another marker. Knit around to the point where you want the second sleeve opening and repeat.

Continue knitting your sweater in the round, knitting the extra stitches every row. If you're using a textured pattern, knit the extra stitches in stockinette stitch. If you're using a multicolor pattern, knit the extra stitches with both colors (knit one red, knit one white, for example).

When you've knitted up to the shoulders, decrease back to the original four stitches. Graft or purl together your shoulder seams. Now steel yourself, and cut the extra stitches right down the middle, from the shoulder to about 1 inch above where you started the sleeve opening. On circular or double-pointed needles, pick up the sleeve stitches around the opening, ½ inch from the cut edge. The marker stitches will naturally curl in toward the wrong side of the fabric, forming a ½-inch facing. You're ready to knit the sleeve down to the cuff.

I know you won't believe it until you've tried it (I didn't either), but the edges will not unravel. In fact, after a couple of washings, the cut edges will felt and actually become stronger than the knitted fabric.

I didn't invent this technique—it's copied from an old sweater from the north of Norway. I've never tried it with any yarn other than wool, so if you'd like to try it with cotton or man-made fibers, test the yarn you're using by knitting and cutting a tube first.

— *Carol Gordon, Staten Island, NY*

Facings instead of steeks

Here is my method of knitting in the round without steeks. When I come to each underarm, I place 8 percent of the body stitches on a scrap of yarn (Elizabeth Zimmermann's percentage system). I then cast on the desired number of stitches for the armhole facings, adding a few extra stitches if I'm not using wool, and I continue knitting around.

When I get to the top of the armhole, I bind off the facing stitches and join the shoulder. This gives me a one-piece facing of knit fabric that is not attached at the top or bottom. I machine-stitch two rows down the center of the piece, stretching while stitching so as not to restrict the fabric's give. With wool, this stitching is unnecessary.

Next, I pick up the sleeve stitches around the armhole and the underarm stitches from the holder. I get a nice, round armhole, and the sleeve is easy to work. When it's finished, I cut between the two rows of machine stitches to open the armhole. The tiny stitches prevent unraveling, and since I don't have to roll the facing, there is no bulk.

Aran in the round

I understand that an Aran sweater was traditionally worked as a seamless garment, though both constructions produce credible sweaters. However, for yarn knitters in the round (courtesy of my old copy of *Mon Tricot),* cast on double-pointed needles stitches for the neck and work around to the desired length. Add a saddle on either side (back and forth). Then pick up stitches and work front and back to armhole depth, at which point you work in the round to the waistband. Last, pick up around the armholes and knit the sleeves around.

— *Jean Margolis*

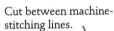

Fig. 122

Cut between machine-stitching lines.

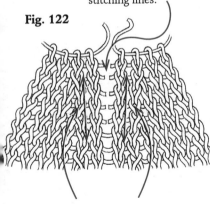

Pick up for neckband along these lines.

V-neck in the round

When I lived in Norway, I learned to knit sweaters in the round (mostly without patterns). It's hard for me to understand why anyone would go to the trouble of making steeks in circular knitting when you can shape armholes and necklines, even V-necks, without them. Here's one trick I learned for putting a V-neck in a drop-shoulder sweater:

Knit the body of the sweater up to about an inch before the point of your V-to-be.

Calculate the number and spacing of stitches needed to decrease on each side of the V.

When you get to the V, decrease as required on both sides of two center-front stitches, but don't stop knitting in the round. It will look like you're forming a dart, but trust me, this works. When you get to the shoulder, stop and put all your stitches on a loose string holder with the string ends at the center-front line. Machine-stitch two lines with a straight stitch (zigzag stretches the neckline) right down the center between the two center-front stitches to the point of the V. Coat both lines of stitching lightly with Fray Check™. When dry, cut between the two lines of machine stitching *(Fig. 122).* Now machine-stitch and cut your armholes, using Fray Check in the same way. Kitchener-stitch the shoulders, then set in and stitch the sleeves. Pick up stitches for your neckband and knit it twice as wide as you want it. Bind off, fold the band to the inside, and hand-stitch it over the raw edge. No steeks to weave in, no balls of yarn getting tangled, no yarn waste. *Det var det!* ("That's that," in Norwegian.)

— *Beth Kollé, Seattle, WA*

SOCKS, GLOVES, HATS, AND SUCH

Designing socks

No matter what design I choose, I always knit with Fair Isle methods, using only two colors in any one round and carrying yarn for very small intervals. This produces a dense, warm, durable fabric. I also use needles a size or two smaller than I would for a sweater. Because a densely patterned knit will have less stretch than a plain knit, a patterned gauge swatch is very important.

I often knit a plain foot, but if I carry the pattern onto the foot, I knit the sole in a seeding pattern, so it will be dense and durable. I knit heels and toes without a pattern and often change color to make the stitches easier to pick up for reknitting when they wear out.

Pattern and color: Because a sock has much less design space than a sweater, I choose small patterns with frequent repeats—both horizontally and vertically. I often use a single background color throughout to provide visual unity. These two simple guidelines define the perfect framework for experimentation.

The long-lived sock: To keep my socks long-lasting, I wash them often and give them a rest between wearings. When the heels and toes wear out, I either cut the sock off at the foot and reknit the whole foot or reknit the worn-out part. You can reknit a turned heel this way: Cut off the old heel and unravel the yarn until a clear line of stitches is visible. Pick up the heel stitches at the top of the heel. Don't unravel beyond the instep gusset. Work the heel back and forth, picking up stitches on the sides of the heel as you knit to join the new heel to the foot as you go. When the heel flap is long enough, turn the heel normally, leaving the same number of stitches on the heel as on the sole. Graft them together with Kitchener stitch.

— *Peg Richard*

Square-heeled, ribbed socks

I knit a lot of socks, and find that a knit two, purl two rib on the leg and top of the foot fits especially well. Ribbing is stretchy, so I cast on about two-thirds the number of stitches that the stockinette gauge and leg measurement would call for.

I also prefer to knit a "square heel" turn. To turn a square heel, you knit short rows back and forth on the central third of the heel stitches and, at the end of each short row, you knit the last center stitch together with the adjacent side-heel stitch. When you've eliminated all the edge stitches, the center stitches form a right angle to them.

Begin the heel turn by knitting across one-third of the total heel stitches, minus one; knit two together; knit the center third, minus two; knit two together; turn. *Purl the center third, minus one; purl two together; turn. Knit the center third, minus one; knit two together; turn. Repeat from * until exactly one-third of the total heel stitches remain, ending with a wrong-side row.

— *Isobel Morgan, Dubbo, NSW, Australia*

Reinforcing socks

Since I can no longer find nylon heel-and-toe filament, I use silk sewing thread to reinforce the heels and toes of socks when I'm knitting them. It works very well. I also find that I can eliminate stress when turning the corner on gussets by using an extra needle for several rounds. I arrange the stitches with the bottom of the heel on the first needle, one gusset on the second, the instep on the third, and the other gusset on the fourth.

— *Harriet N. Boker, Westerville, OH*

Stay-on booties

My booties, shown in *Fig. 123,* are unusual in that they'll stay on a newborn's feet because of the ribbed construction. I don't know of anyone else who makes them, and since I'm 95, I don't want them to die with me. I knit the booties of Red Heart Wintuk, a three-ply baby yarn, but some of the new washable wool yarns in this size would also work well. They're easiest to knit on a set of five double-pointed needles, size 0, 1, 2, or 3, depending

Fig. 123

on the gauge you desire; but four needles also work.

Here's how I make them: Cast on 10 stitches and knit 18 ridges (36 rows) of garter stitch for the sole. Leave the 10 stitches on one needle, and on a second, pick up 10 stitches at the cast-on edge. Pick up 18 stitches along each side on two more needles—56 stitches in all. Be careful to keep working around in the same direction. Purl 4 rounds, knit 4 rounds, purl 4 rounds, knit 4 rounds, purl 4 rounds.

To shape the toe at one of the 10-stitch ends, knit and purl short rows back and forth. Work the 10th stitch together with the closest stitch on the adjacent 18-stitch needle at the end of each row 16 times (decrease 8 stitches per side). You do this by slipping the 10th stitch to the right needle purlwise, then back onto the 18-stitch needle. Knit or purl the first 2 stitches on the 18-stitch needle together. Then turn and work back across the 10 toe stitches to the other side.

Now knit around the 40 stitches at the ankle for 3 rounds. To prevent a hole at the end of the 1st round, pick up 1 extra stitch and knit it together with the 1st stitch on the 2nd round. Make eyelets for the ties on the 4th round: *K2, yo, k2tog* 10 times. Finally, knit 22 rounds, and bind off. Thread crocheted yarn ties or ribbon through the eyelets.

— *Christine Bourquin, Redwood City, CA*

The world's simplest knitted slippers

Make an extra pair or two of these, shown in *Fig. 124,* for cold winter nights to come. Directions are for women's medium or men's small. For larger sizes, use heavier yarn or

Fig. 124

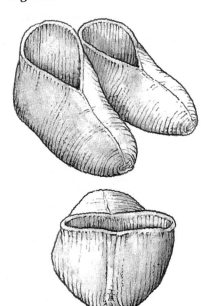

larger needles. Use worsted-weight yarn and size 1, 2, or 3 needles for a firm, tight gauge of about 6 stitches and 6 garter ridges (12 rows) per inch. Cast on 50 stitches, leaving a long end for sewing the heel seam. Work in garter stitch (knit every row), slipping the first stitch of each row for a chain selvage. When the length reaches from the center back of the heel to the end of the little toe, measured along the side of the foot (usually about 8½ inches), begin toe decreases (dec indicates k2tog) on every right-side row as follows:

Row 1:
K9, dec, k3, dec, k18, dec, k3, dec, k9.

Row 3:
K8, dec, k3, dec, k16, dec, k3, dec, k8.

Row 5:
K7, dec, k3, dec, k14, dec, k3, dec, k7.

Row 7:
K6, dec, k3, dec, k12, dec, k3, dec, k6.

Row 9:
K5, dec, k3, dec, k10, dec, k3, dec, k5.

Row 11:
K4, dec, k3, dec, k8, dec, k3, dec, k4.

Row 13:
K3, dec, k3, dec, k6, dec, k3, dec, k3.

Row 15:
K2, dec, k3, dec, k4, dec, k3, dec, k2.

Bind off the remaining 18 stitches. Finish by folding the cast-on edge in half, sewing the back heel seam down to the fold, and tying the last 6 stitches all together. Beginning at the toe, sew the side edges together halfway up the instep, leaving enough space to insert your foot. With a separate thread, sew across the toe opening.

Make the second slipper like the first. To be sure they're both the same size, count the garter-stitch rows and mark the ridge where the decreases begin, or work both slippers at the same time on the same needle with two separate skeins of yarn.

— *Barbara G. Walker, Morristown, NJ*

Quick cord maker

My husband devised an inexpensive, quick cord maker that I use to make belts, drawstrings, and straps for the garments I hand-weave. Some basic woodworking skills and a few tools are required to make this gadget. It consists of a plywood disk with eye screws that is attached to the front end of a drill *(Fig. 125)*. The yarn is attached to the eye screws and to dowels that are clamped to a secure surface. When the drill is turned on, the yarn is wound to make a tight plied cord of any length or thickness.

Decide on the length of your finished cord, multiply that number by 4½ or 5, and cut a guide cord to that length. (Use the yarn you'll use for the finished cord as the guide cord.) Insert the disk's center bolt into the drill-bit socket and attach the dowel clamp to a sturdy piece of furniture. Tie one end of the guide cord to one of the dowels and loop the midpoint of the yarn strand around one of the hooks on the disk. Tie the other end of the strand to the other dowel. This will give

Fig. 125

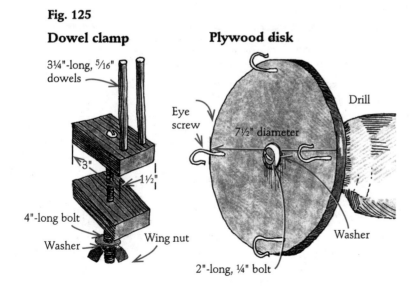

Dowel clamp

3¼"-long, ⁵⁄₁₆" dowels

3"

1½"

4"-long bolt

Washer

Wing nut

Plywood disk

Drill

Eye screw

7½" diameter

Washer

2"-long, ¼" bolt

you twice the length of the finished cord.

Now hook the yarn for the finished cord around two, three, or four of the eye screws (for a small amount of yarn, I use only two hooks), and wrap it back around the dowels. Continue until you have half the desired thickness of the cord when you squeeze the strands close together. (Note: If you use only two hooks, make sure they are opposite each other in order to keep the winding balanced.)

Run the drill until the yarn is wound tight. Then grab the cord at its center, double it back, and place the disk behind the dowel clamp, keeping the cord taut (have someone help you). Let the cord twist back on itself slowly. Be sure to knot the ends near the dowels before cutting the cord away from the tools.

— *Jane Taubensee, Bloomington, IN*

Knitted finger puppets

The quickest and cutest knitted toys I've seen can be off your needles and entertaining youngsters in a matter of minutes. They're tiny pull-on hats with faces underneath that just fit your fingertips. Here's the basic recipe (if you enjoy making them, you'll soon find lots of variations): With baby yarn and size 2, 3, or 4 needles, cast on 15 stitches in a color suitable for your character's face. Work stockinette stitch for about ⅝ inch. Break the yarn and start again in whatever color you want for the hat, knitting two or three rows in garter stitch, then changing back to stockinette. When the hat measures ½ to ¾ inches, cut the yarn, leaving an 8-inch tail. Thread the tail through the 15 stitches, then embroider features onto the center of the face. Pull up the stitches on the thread to close the top, sew up the back seam with the remaining thread, and start another puppet so your little person will have someone to talk to.

— *Mimi Nelson, Trotwood, OH*

A doormat from large-scale knitting

Here's a method for knitting a durable doormat. You'll need a whole spool (380 feet) of 3/16-inch nylon rope. (Be sure to ask the hardware store for a discount since you're buying the whole spool.) For size 13 knitting needles, cut a 36-inch-long, 3/8-inch-diameter dowel in half. You do not have to make points on the needles. Mark the end of one needle; this needle will be used throughout for all shaping (increasing and decreasing), which occurs on only the right-side rows.

The mat is a bias-knit rectangle, as shown in *Fig. 126*. Cast on 2 stitches with the unmarked needle (this is the wrong side and from this point on you'll just knit all the stitches of every WS row). Turn to the

Fig. 126

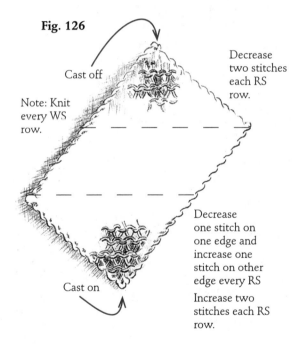

Cast off

Decrease two stitches each RS row.

Note: Knit every WS row.

Decrease one stitch on one edge and increase one stitch on other edge every RS row

Increase two stitches each RS row.

Cast on

right side. With the marked needle, k1, yo, k1; turn. With the unmarked needle, k1, k1 into the back of the yo loop, k1; turn. With the marked needle, k1, yo, k1, yo, k1. Continue increasing on every RS row until a side of the knitting equals the short side of the desired size mat, using another mat to measure. Then knit the midsection of the mat, increasing with a yo after the first stitch and decreasing at the end of every RS row to maintain the same number of stitches in each row. To decrease, knit up to the last 2 sts, sl 1 st pwise, k1, psso.

Knit the midsection until the length of the long side equals that of the mat, then begin decreasing at each end of the RS rows as follows: Sl 1 pwise, k1, psso. Knit to the last 2 sts, sl 1 pwise, k1, psso. Decrease to 3 sts, knit the WS row, decrease to 2 sts (RS row), and cast off. Cut the rope and sear the end with a lit match to prevent fraying. Work in both ends of rope.

— *Therese M. Inverso, Camden, NJ*

FIVE

MANAGING YOUR KNITTING

Needle Notes

Keeping on Track
With Knitting

Patterns

Joining Yarn

Tool Management
and Storage

Tool Substitution

Odds and Ends

NEEDLE NOTES

Simplified swatch notes

Instead of recording the needle size used for your knitting swatch on a paper label, tie an appropriate number of knots in the tail of yarn left over from casting on—seven knots means needle size 7.

—*Barbara Shomer Kelsey, Bethel, CT*

Teaching beginning knitters

When teaching beginners to knit, give them two same-size needles that are different colors. People who have no trouble distinguishing left from right under normal circumstances can get very confused when they're first learning to knit. It's much easier to tell a beginner how to move her blue needle in relation to her red one than to force her to think about left and right in addition to the new skill she's acquiring.

—*Ellen Shaffer, Minneapolis, MN*

Hand knitting as even as machine knitting

I've found that European knitters often use a size smaller needle on the purl side of stockinette stitch than on the knit side. The overall effect is as even as machine knitting with no unsightly spaces between every other row. There's hardly any effect on gauge. One or two extra rows are all I ever need to compensate.

—*Billie Gooding, Hugo, OK*

Detachable needle tips for tight knitting

Tight knitting can make fancy bobble stitches (knit three in a single stitch) difficult to knit because the stitch on the left needle needs to be loose to execute the stitch easily. The use of circular needles with detachable, replaceable tips, found in Boyle® needle sets, can solve the problem if you use two different needle tip sizes. Attach a tip the correct gauge to the right needle and a tip two or three sizes smaller to the left needle. The smaller tip makes it possible to knit several stitches together and still knit the finished bobble or other multiple stitch onto the gauge needle without difficulty. Straight-needle knitters can use this trick by sliding the work onto a smaller needle to knit a bobble, but knitting it onto the needle size needed to obtain gauge.

—*Josephine W. Boyd, Fort Collins, CO*

KEEPING ON TRACK WITH KNITTING PATTERNS

Compact stitch instructions

I find it convenient to carry my crochet or knitting instructions written on 3- by 5-inch index cards. First I reinforce the edge of the card with tape, and punch a hole next to the instructions for each row or round. I put a safety pin in the hole by the row I am working as a marker. When I need to pack up and go, I attach the safety pin and pattern to the loop of the stitch I am working.

—*Anna-Lisa Kanick, Tacoma, WA*

Keep it on one page

Complete knitting directions for complex patterns almost never appear on a single page of the instruction booklet. I copy the directions from the various pages, cut them up into pieces, and paste the pieces onto a single sheet of 8½-inch by 11-inch paper. Then I clip these to cardboard for easy handling. I also find it easier to write notes on the sheets than on the polished surface of the booklet paper.

—*Mary M. Lund, Arlington, WA*

Following a difficult pattern

I write each row on a metal board with magnetic strips (the kind used for cross-stitch) and position the strip under the row I'm knitting.

—*Lynn Teichman, Lewisburg, PA*

Put it on index cards

When knitting a sweater that has many different rows to the pattern, I use a simple method to keep track of what row I am working on.

I write out each row on a 3- by 5-inch index card and put the row number in one corner. I stack the cards numerically and clip them together. As I finish each row, I put its card on the bottom of the stack. The next row on top is the next row to be done. This is much easier than following a pattern book.

Some stores carry 3- by 5-inch index cards on a ring binder. This is even better. I flip the card when each row is done and hold my place with a paper clip or an elastic band.
—*Mrs. Robert Carlson, Auburn, MA*

Listen to your knitting pattern

Knitting an intricate pattern, such as a lace, that requires frequent references to a printed page can become tiresome after a while. Record the pattern on an audiocassette and replay it as you knit. You're less likely to lose your concentration and your place in the row.
—*Sara Tayloe, Arvada, CO*

Click your count

I like to knit lace, but I used to find it most difficult to keep track of rows or rounds until I saw a person clicking off people going through a gate. I went right out and found my own "people clicker."
—*Mary Haverlandt, San Diego, CA*

Marking a pattern

I recently used a Post-it® Note to mark the rows on my knitting chart. Placed either above or below the line I was on, it was easy to see and move. I liked it even better than my magnet strips.
—*Mary Bright, Cuyahoga Falls, OH*

Easy-to-read Fair Isle knitting charts

Keeping your place while knitting Fair Isle can be a chore. Consider those complex predesigned charts where each color is represented by a different symbol. All those symbols jumble together in small squares. How do you sort out the repeats and what the designs look like, and how do you keep your place?

I enlarge the pattern on a copy machine. If it's long, I divide it in half and put it on two sheets of paper. For easy viewing, I divide the pattern evenly into groups of about 8 to 10 stitches each with colored vertical lines. For a row guide, I cut a piece of 1-inch-wide tacky paper tape equal to the width of the pattern, drawing colored lines through the tape to match the pattern. The tape can be moved up the rows easily but will stay put above the row being worked on. For needle markers as I knit, I use loops of embroidery floss that correspond to the vertical color lines drawn on the graph. If I'm knitting a large-size sweater on circular needles, I use many colored markers. But at a glance, I can still tell where I am in my knitting.

—*Helen T. Healy, Lincoln, MA*

Color in those charts

I found I was spending a lot of time checking which color went with which letter or symbol on my black-and-white knitting charts. Now I start my project by coloring the diagram with colored pencils, so I can see at a glance when to change colors.

—*Ethel Roberts, Berkeley, CA*

Make your own chart

Using graph paper and crayons, I make my own knitting chart, which is easier to read than published charts. I number the rows and include my own color key and any helpful notes. To keep my place, I put the chart in a plastic page protector with a cardboard guide clipped to the chart, which I then move up the outside of the chart as I complete each row.

—*Evelyn B. Coyne, Wickliffe, OH*

Customized knitting guide sheets

When I've designed a sweater using stitch patterns and ideas assembled from various sources and want an easy-to-carry guide, I gather all my reference materials and head for the copy shop, where I photocopy each element I need for the garment: gauge, a schematic drawing of the garment, charts, directions, photos of stitches, and any notes, reducing them if necessary so they'll all fit on a single sheet of paper. Then I assemble all the parts, paste them up, and copy the whole thing. Uncomplicated designs can usually fit on one side of regular- or legal-size paper, making a handy permanent record.

—*Jean Margolis, Sebastopol, CA*

Keeping track of knitting

I usually design my own knit or crochet project, so I don't need complete directions for shaping, finishing off, etc., but often I want to keep a record of a particular stitch to use in the future. I type out the directions on a 4- by 6-inch index card, then make up a swatch showing one or two repeats (about 2 by 3 inches). I staple the swatch to the back of the card to jog my memory.

    —Olive Crook, Green Bay, WI

Counting rows

If you have trouble counting rows, turn your work to the purl side, where the rows are more clearly defined. And don't be afraid to stretch your knitting. Pull it from the top to bottom to separate the rows. Counting rows is more important than some people might think. If you've knit a 10-row pocket, for example, you should sew it row-for-row onto 10 rows of your sweater front. And if you have two pockets that you want six rows up from the ribbing, count those rows so that the two pockets will be even.

JOINING YARN
How to splice yarn

Instead of using knots when I'm knitting or crocheting, I splice the yarns. Here's how I do it.

Step 1: Separate the plies of one strand of yarn *(Fig. 127)*.

Step 2: Thread one ply into the eye of a needle *(Fig. 128)*.

Step 3: Weave the needle through about 1½ to 2 inches of a second strand of yarn *(Fig. 129)*.

Step 4: Repeat the procedure for each remaining ply. Trim off all the protruding ends *(Fig. 130)*. This makes a strong splice that will not show in the finished work

    —Lois Albrecht, Stoddard, WI

Starting and ending yarns

The way I join in a new skein of the same color yarn when I'm knitting or crocheting makes a nearly invisible join. It's especially helpful with a single yarn that can't be spliced. I knit until 3 or 4 inches remain of the old yarn. I lay the new yarn against the

Fig. 127

Fig. 128

Fig. 129

Fig. 130

wrong side of my work, next to the last stitch I knit, leaving a 2- to 3-inch end. Now, doubling the yarns of the old and new skeins together, I knit three or four stitches, then continue knitting on with only the new yarn. Later, weaving the ends into the back of the work will secure the join permanently. In this way, the join can be made anywhere along the row because the doubled stitches will settle invisibly into the work, leaving a completely smooth and attractive surface. I break the ends of natural-fiber yarns instead of cutting them. This produces a frayed end, and the individual fibers will interlock with the fibers of the fabric when the ends are later woven into the wrong side of the piece.

—*Charlene Rose, Marblemount, WA*

Invisible yarn-ball change

When knitting lace patterns, a good way to start a new ball of yarn and hide the change is in a decrease. On the row before you are to work a k2tog, work the first stitch with the old ball, then the next stitch with the new ball. Tie a temporary square knot with the loose ends. In the following row, knit the two stitches together, which stabilizes the yarn change and makes it invisible. When your project is complete, untie the square knot, twist the yarns together in a half-turn, and rock the ends into the decrease cross to secure them.

—*Susan L. Terry, Orlando, FL*

TOOL MANAGEMENT AND STORAGE

Relaxation tip for circular needles

A soak in hot water loosens up a coiled circular knitting needle.

—*Beth Kollé, Seattle, WA*

Taming circular needles

When you are about to begin a new project, hold the needle outstretched, one hand near each point, under very hot running water, moving the needle back and forth through the water. Occasionally remove it from the stream and straighten it further by running your fingers across its entire length. Within a short time, all of the tension will be eased, and the needle will work perfectly.

—*Bess Kuzma, Trenton, NJ*

Point protectors for four-needle knitting

After trying many ways of securing four-needle sets when making socks and mittens, I finally solved the problem by buying point protectors for large needles. The packet I bought held two extra-large flexible point protectors for 4 mm to 7 mm needles (approximately U.S. sizes 6 to 10½ or English sizes 8 to 2). Each protector will fit over the ends of four small needles, ranging from about 2.25 mm to 3 mm (U.S. sizes 1 to 3 or English sizes 13 to 10).

—*L. Manton, Montreal, PQ, Canada*

Easy-to-find needle protectors

To keep from losing my knitting needle protectors, I connect them with a length of yarn stitched through the rubber tips and knotted at the ends. Use a stout needle and leave just enough yarn between the tips so you can use them normally. When the protectors fall, they don't go far. Besides, a pair is easier to find.

—*Betty Isaacson, Vancouver, WA*

Easy-to-find cable needle

To prevent losing my small U-shaped cable needle when it's not in use, I anchor it in the sweater by securing its short end with a point protector.

—*Linda Van Houten, Juneau, AK*

Knitting tools pouch

I regularly knit while taking public transportation to and from work and often lose things in my knitting bag. I solved my problem by putting all my equipment (except for the yarn and needles)—a 6-inch ruler, a crochet hook for dropped stitches, folding scissors, stitch markers, cable needles, and needle guards—into a sandwich-size zip-top plastic bag. Now I can always find what I need, and I can easily replace the bag when it tears or becomes soiled.

—*Joan M. Harris, Pullman, WA*

Fig. 131

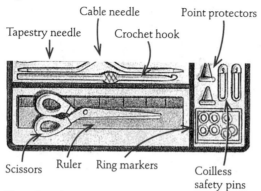

Tapestry needle · Cable needle · Crochet hook · Point protectors

Scissors · Ruler · Ring markers · Coilless safety pins

Use a dental organizer to carry your knitting gadgets neatly and safely.

Fig. 132

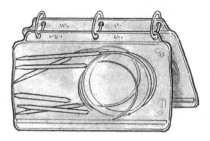

Knitter's gadget organizer

I use a dental organizer to hold my small knitting gadgets *(Fig. 131)*. This plastic case, which I bought at a local drugstore, easily fits into a purse and is at least child-deterring. It comes in some wonderfully bright colors.

— *Pamela Staveley, Bena, VA*

Circular-needle storage

Commercial organizers for circular knitting needles just don't suit me. Instead, I store them in clear plastic sheet protectors from my stationery store *(Fig. 132)*. The sheets are closed on three sides and open at the top. They have a strip on the side with holes for placing in a binder. Once I label the envelope with the needle size and slide my circular needles inside, I have permanent, see-through storage for my collection.

— *Peg Boren, McAllen, TX*

A circular needle file

I use an accordion file folder with multiple pockets (9½ by 7½ inches, found in office-supply stores) to hold my circular needles and keep them organized. The pockets can be labeled, and each will hold all the lengths of a single size, plus small double-pointed needles. It even has an attached elastic band to keep everything secure just in case it overturns.

— *Beth La Breche, Fridley, MN*

Circular-needle holder

I made my own storage holder for circular needles from a 2-inch by 1-yard strip of notched cardboard folded in half *(Fig. 133)*. Rubber bands around the notches hold the layers together. My needles slip easily between the layers of the compartments, which I've numbered with the needles' sizes. I made two holders—one for short needles and one for long ones—which hang on separate hangers in my sewing-room closet.

— *Eve Sobery, Florissant, MO*

Portable circular-needle storage

Here's how to make an inexpensive portable circular-needle holder: Start with two 17- by 8-inch rectangles of denim (any heavyweight fabric will do). Quilt the back panel to pad the holder. Sew a 2-yard-long, 2-inch-wide strip of grosgrain ribbon into loops down the center of the front panel. Use your needles as a guide for the loop sizes, and a zipper foot to sew close to them *(Fig. 134)*. Knit rectangular seed-stitch pockets to punch the points through, and stitch the pockets to the front panel. Add three small pockets on the bottom to hold accessories. My panels were sewn wrong sides together (you can also bind the panels together on the edges). Add crocheted ties to secure the sides when the holder is folded in half, and attach two metal rings at the top to hang it up.

— *Jean W. Jeppson, Midvale, UT*

Fig. 133

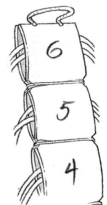

Fig. 134

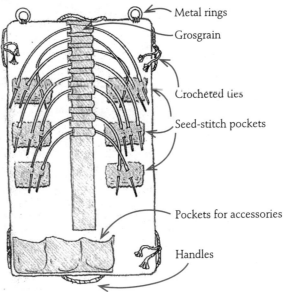

Metal rings

Grosgrain

Crocheted ties

Seed-stitch pockets

Pockets for accessories

Handles

Storing circular needles

Zip-top plastic bags are ideal for storing circular knitting needles, one per bag. The bags come in various sizes to accommodate the different needle lengths. I put self-adhesive labels on the bags to show the needle sizes and the lengths, and then I file the needles in numerical order for quick retrieval.

— *Sara Tayloe, Arvada, CO*

Make a circular needle book

With a standard three-hole loose-leaf binder and 1-gallon resealable plastic bags, you can make a great organizer for a collection of circular needles, or anything else that'll fit into the bags. Reinforce the bottom of the bags by folding them over twice and machine-stitching the fold with a long stitch and a size 14 needle (I marked each bag at 8½ inches from the opening and folded to the line to make them all the size I wanted).

With an ordinary hole punch, make holes through the folded layers, and label each bag with a permanent marker or by slipping paper labels into them. Each bag will hold several different lengths of the same size needles.

— *Sandee Jaastad, Denver, CO*

Keeping track of circular needle sizes

Are your circular knitting needles in a jumble? Mine were. Now, to tell at a glance which needle is what size, I slip one of those plastic bread-closure clips on each needle. I print the needle's size and length on the back of the clip in large letters with a water-proof pen.

— *Kathleen C. Saxe, Sioux City, IA*

TOOL SUBSTITUTION
Knitters' measuring aid

To avoid constant measuring when I knit, I mark the work with a length of thin, nonstretchy yarn, like pearl cotton, a few inches longer than the distance to be knitted. I tie an overhand knot at one end, leaving a loop that fits around the needle, and connect the other end to the knitting, as shown in *Fig. 135*. I adjust the distance between the two connections to the length of knitting required. When the slack is gone, I've knitted far enough.

— *Ninon deZara/Ronn, Roxbury, CT*

Fig. 135

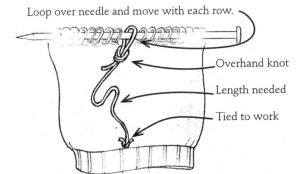

Loop over needle and move with each row.

Overhand knot

Length needed

Tied to work

Ribbon stitch holder

Recently I knit a hat for my little boy and wanted to try it on him when I'd finished the ribbing. I used a piece of narrow satin ribbon instead of yarn to hold the stitches. Even though my yarn was very fuzzy, the stitches slipped onto the ribbon easily. And having the ribbon to "scoop" against made replacing the stitches on the knitting needles a snap.

— *Ann Miller, Flagstaff, AZ*

Cable holders

I always use a safety pin to twist the cables in knitting. It is small enough not to get in the way and can be parked and retrieved easily in the work without even unwinding yarn from my fingers. At the end of the row I pin it into the bottom of the knitting so it's never lost.

— *Margaret Horton, Atlanta, GA*

Fig. 136

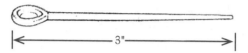

|←——————— 3" ———————→|

Another alternative

It's so easy to lose a double-pointed cable knitting needle. After trying several alternatives, including toothpicks, I bought a package of plastic hair-roller picks (the pins used with brush rollers—*Fig. 136.* The small knob on one end keeps the pick from sliding through the knitting, where I park it. This knob also secures cabled stitches on the needle, as long as the point is placed downward. The knob is small enough that the stitches can be pulled over it after they have been knitted.

— *Carol L. Douglas, Phoenix, AZ*

Glove needles

While knitting a pair of fine-gauge stranded gloves, I became very frustrated with manipulating four regular-length double-pointed needles. I asked around for glove needles but had no luck. In desperation, I bought a pair of 16-inch-long single-pointed size 0 bamboo needles at a local craft store. I used a mat knife to cut one needle into six 2½-inch segments. Then I shaped points on each end of the short pieces and lightly sprayed my new glove needles with a clear matte finish to prevent the ends from splitting.

The needles were a delight to work with. Because I could easily make a spare, I didn't become frantic over lost needles. When I was done, I stored them in a small plastic box along with the remains of the original needle and bought more bamboo needles in other sizes to cut down for other glove needles.

— *Susan A. Lupton, Indian Hills, CO*

Custom knitting needles

I have an easy way to make my own knitting needles in any length I need from white birch dowels. As the chart on the facing page shows, standard dowel sizes don't correspond to every needle size, but I find these sizes useful.

Equivalent Needle Size

Dowel diameter (inches)	U.S.	Metric
⅛	3	3.25
³⁄₁₆	6	4
¼	10½	6.5
⁵⁄₁₆	11	7
⅜	13	8

Cut the dowels to the length you desire (I use anything from 6 to 36 inches), and sharpen one end in a pencil sharpener or with a knife. Sand the needle, especially the end, to remove burrs and smooth the wood. It's important to do a very thorough job of this. Rub the sanded needles with paraffin wax, which will make the yarn slide nicely for easier knitting. To keep the yarn on the needles, I suggest either wrapping a rubber band around the blunt end several times or gluing on a button.

— *Charlie Collins, Virgin, UT*

Cut up straws for stitch markers

Thin rings cut from a plastic drinking straw make lightweight, easy-to-create knitting markers that don't slip through the stitches. When I have more than one marker on a needle, I put a colored thread through one of the circles to show which is which.

— *Brigitte Harris, Powell River, BC, Canada*

Rubber O-rings as stitch markers

Slit-ring stitch markers would often catch my knitting yarn. To avoid entanglement, I would have to slow down when coming up to a marker. I never once had the occasion to use the slit feature, which is for adding or removing the marker when it isn't at the needle point. I now use rubber O-rings from the hardware store. They come in a variety of sizes and are unbroken loops. Being rubber, they don't break and can hold up to speedy knitting. They are a bit more expensive, but I am happy to pay the price.

— *Martha Jaffe, Kensington, MD*

Clip it!

Colored paper clips are excellent for marking hand knitting, especially for complicated texture patterns, which are hard to see when the knitting hasn't progressed much beyond the ribbing. I usually knit on circular needles, so I mark center front and back and side seams, each with a different color clip. Then I mark each side of every pattern section again with its own color. Until the patterns become apparent at a glance, the clips can be easily moved up as needed.

— *Dorothy Bird, Guemes Island, WA*

Change the color with the stitch

I like to mark my knitting by slipping a bobby pin over certain stitches. I use a black bobby pin for each increase and a silver one for decrease stitches. You could also use a spot of fingernail polish on the bobby pin to indicate whatever you have trouble remembering.

— *Jean Scheffler, Shelbyville, IN*

Fig. 137

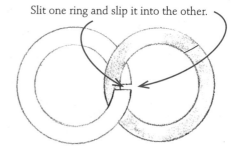

Slit one ring and slip it into the other.

Two-row knitting marker

I have found the hybrid marker shown in *Fig. 137* to be helpful in circular knitting where shaping is done on alternate rounds (like a raglan sweater knit from the neck down). Instead of trying to remember which kind of row I'm on, I use two colors of marker rings. I slit one with a craft knife and slip it into the other, then pick up the free ring on every round. For me, red means "stop and increase," and green means "go on knitting," but the color isn't important as long as you remember which is which. Yarn loops would work as well.

— *Lisa Mannery, Seattle, WA*

Yarn markers

Use scraps of yarn (about 5 inches long) as markers in your knitting—within the row to mark pattern changes, like the beginning of cables, or at the edges of the row to mark increases, etc. Lay the yarn along the completed stitch and knit over it.

I'm knitting a garment whose instructions read, "*Increase every 4th row twice, every 6th row once*. Repeat between *'s 5 times." This means increasing in every 4th row 10 times, and in every 6th row 5 times. I cut 10 lengths of one color to mark every 4th-row increase and 5 lengths of another color to mark the 6th-row increases. When I come back to my work, I can see immediately what I've done last—no need for notes. When the yarn markers are all used, my increase sequence is complete—no need to count or keep track.

Yarn markers are flexible, stay where they're put, are easily removed with a pull, and are free. Avoid strongly contrasting markers with lots of fuzzies—they'll leave telltale fibers.

— *Elizabeth Rothman, Seattle, WA*

Marking cables in the round with yarn

When I make an Aran sweater in the round, I use 3- to 4-inch pieces of a contrasting color yarn to mark the turning rows. I simply hang the yarn between two stitches just before turning a cable. The piece of yarn stays put but out of my way and lets me count how many rows I have done between turns.

— *Josette M. Kilmer, Rancho Palos Verdes, CA*

Counting stitches with yarn

When you have a lot of stitches on your knitting that you will need to count, weave a contrasting yarn in every 10 stitches as you knit the row before. That way, if you have to stop, it's easier to resume counting just a few stitches (fewer than 10) than to start all over.

— *Josette M. Kilmer, Rancho Palos Verdes, CA*

Recycle twist ties

I use plastic closures or ties from bread or produce bags for yarn markers. It's an inexpensive, surefire way to mark increases, decreases, or changes in the pattern. These closures clip on and off easily and won't pull or snag the yarn. I keep mine in a zip-top plastic bag and use them over and over.

— *Sue Fruth, Clearwater, MN*

Knitting row counter

I like to use the barrel-type row counter, but it leaves a large gap when knitting in the round. I solved this problem by putting a bead chain (like a key chain) through the counter and slipping the chain over the needle. Now every time I come to the chain, I turn the numbers one notch.

— *Susan Terry, Orlando, FL*

ODDS AND ENDS

Knitting in close quarters

If you're going to be knitting while traveling, especially on an airplane or a bus, it's much easier to knit on circular needles than on straight ones. They take up less elbow room and less space in your bag. You don't need a pattern designed for circular needles, just knit back and forth in the usual way, as if you had two separate needles.

— *Ruth S. Galpin, Southport, CT*

Stopping midrow

We have all been told never to stop in the middle of a row of knitting. Rather than ripping back to the beginning or hurrying through to the end of the row (and maybe making a mistake), just slip the stitches from the needle with the fewer number of stitches to the one with the greater number. Slipping stitches is much quicker than knitting them, especially if you are working with a pattern. When you pick up your knitting again, just slip those stitches back onto the proper needle. The yarn attached to your skein will tell you where you left off.

— *Gail Dunleavy, West Grove, PA*

Keep it clean

When I crochet, knit, or work on my miniatures, I work off a tray table covered with a large, soft, thin "country cotton" towel. When I lay my work down, I cover it with the ends of the clean towel, and it stays put, despite our eight cats.

— *Nancy Kelly, Brooksville, FL*

Photocopying textiles

Photocopies of lace, knitting, crochet, macrame, and other textiles are beautiful, easy to make, and have many uses. You can run off multiple copies of a motif in a wink and use them to create new designs that can themselves be copied for further experimentation. Photocopies are excellent to record your own or borrowed work, analyze stitches, reckon gauge, or share ideas. For classes, nothing compares with instructions accompanied by a life-size photocopy of the project. Copies of your work on good paper are impressive to include with show applications and queries to publishers and to hand out as brochures and samples for customers. These ideas are just the tip of a promising iceberg.

When placed on the copier window, light-colored yarns need a black background, so cover the piece with black cloth, construction paper, or mat board big enough to cover the window. Play with the light-dark settings. If you can find a copier that reduces and enlarges, the possibilities are endless.

— *Ruby Moore, Tallahassee, FL*

Self-indexing

I subscribe to several different knitting-related magazines and was getting tired of flipping through so many back issues looking for that special idea I'd once read about. So I created a personal index using a business-card file. When a new issue comes in with something I want to remember, I write out a card and file it alphabetically according to topic. I note the magazine, date, and pages. This little extra effort has really saved time and frustration.

— *Marydee Sklar, Portland, OR*

Document your work

Always take photographs of your finished projects. In time you will have an album full of accomplishments to look back on, and a handy reference when duplicating a past project.

— *Karen McCormic, Many, LA*

SIX

MACHINE KNITTING

Casting On and Maintaining Tension

Increases, Decreases, and Tucks

Machine-Knitting Techniques

Binding Off and Managing Your Ends

Seams and Necklines

Odds and Ends

CASTING ON AND MAINTAINING TENSION

Casting on yarn

Machine knitters often cast on with a few rows of waste yarn, then switch to knitting with the fashion yarn if they plan to pick up the open stitches of the fashion yarn later and machine- or hand-knit a ribbing or other edging. The waste yarn is removed in the finishing process. It holds the stitches until they're needed, at which time you clip and pull out the last row of waste yarn. The rest of the waste yarn falls off, leaving stitches ready for picking up and knitting (Fig. 138).

Use a smooth, strong yarn that is finer than the fashion yarn, which makes it easier to remove. Leftover cones of 5/2 pearl cotton are appropriate; even fine, strong cotton string on cones (sometimes available in hardware stores) can serve as a wonderful, inexpensive waste yarn. Waste yarn doesn't have to be on cones. Leftover balls of yarn can also be used, although they tend to be smaller and require more frequent replacing than cones, and they tend to tangle more easily.

Firm beginnings for machine knitters

It's usually how well the details are carried off that makes one garment look more professional than another. If you're a typical double-bed machine knitter, one of the details that you'd most like to improve is your rib cast-ons. Many knitters, especially those with chunky-gauge machines, complain that their cast-on edges tend to be saggy and loose.

The problem is often worse when you're trying to knit with your machine's smallest stitch sizes, as you would with lightweight four-ply worsted or heavy sport-weight yarn on a machine with 8-mm or 9-mm needle spacing. When you're planning to knit the body as stitch size 2 or 3, you don't have much room to tighten the ribbing stitches with the tension dial alone.

While no one method will be correct in every situation, there are certain functions we can expect cast-on edges to perform—they should be able to stretch with the rib, return to shape, and help define the edge of the knitting.

Preparing to cast on: Most rib cast-ons are in trouble right after the first zigzag row because the required comb and weights will

Fig. 138

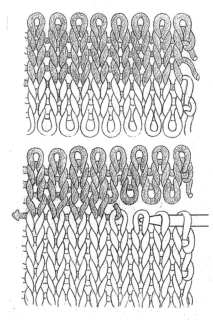

stretch them, however slightly, as soon as they're hung. The easiest way to avoid this is to begin with scrap yarn so the comb and weights never touch the garment. Choose a smooth yarn the same size as your main yarn and set the carriages to a stitch size in the middle range. Knit the first row, hang the comb and weights, then knit about 10 rows so the comb disappears between the beds. Rethread the carriage with ravel cord or a smooth, strong cotton, and knit two circular rows (i.e., one row on each bed) by setting each carriage to knit in one direction and slip in the other.

It takes a few extra moments to do, but I do this for all double-bed casting-on. It saves the beginning edge from the distortion of the comb, and because no comb is in the way, I can work with smaller stitch sizes for the actual cast-on regardless of the tension setting. The circular rows of ravel cord pull out easily later on. You can apply the same technique to neckline edges that you're knitting from the top.

Once the preparation rows are in place, cast on any way you like. The methods I use most often are the basic tubular cast-on, the e-wrap cast-on, and the double, backed-up e-wrap. The tubular and the e-wrap are suitable for both standard and chunky-gauge machines. I use the tubular cast-on when I want to thread elastic through the edge to act as a memory for yarns like cotton and silk, which tend to lose their shape. The e-wrap looks a lot like a handknit cast-on. The double, backed-up e-wrap produces a decorative, braided effect that is especially effective with the chunkies because it adds body and support to edges that might otherwise seem too soft. The tubular cast-on can be applied to knit two, purl two ribbing, but the e-wrap and double, backed-up e-wrap work best with knit one, purl one ribbing.

Tubular cast-on: After completing the scrap-yarn and revel-cord rows, rethread the carriage with the main yarn, set the stitch dials on both carriages to the smallest available stitch size, and set the cams to knit in both directions. Then knit the first row. Follow this with two circular rows (one on each bed). You don't need to bother with the comb; it's already in place. Reset the carriages to knit in both directions, and set the appropriate levers to knit the needles back from holding position. *Bring all the needles to holding position, raise the stitch size by one number, and knit one row**. Repeat from * to ** until you've reached the stitch size you want for the ribbing.

Because the carriages need to knit the needles back from hold only, you can knit on a very small stitch size without fear of breaking or stretching the yarn. Pushing the needles through the stitches by hand is easier on the yarn than using the carriage. When combined with raising the stitch size one number per row, this extra care will greatly reduce the tendency of the finished edge to flare. If the yarn I'm using is particularly inelastic (cotton) or fragile (angora), I continue to bring the needles out to holding position before each row even after I'm up to gauge. It does add another step, but there usually aren't that many rows of ribbing to worry about, and it seems like a small price to pay for the assurance that all the stitches will be perfect.

E-wrap cast-on: Start with the scrap and ravel preparation rows. With the carriages on the right, drop the main yarn between the beds and tie it to the clamp on the left side. Push the first needle forward so the ravel-cord stitch that it holds opens the latch and slides back on its shaft. Make an e-wrap in the hook of the needle, then push the needle back to knit the wrap through the ravel-cord stitch.

— *Susan Guagliumi*

Using the waste yarn

As a new machine knitter, I've been bothered by the tangled waste yarn pulled from each garment. Now I cut a 3- by 4-inch bobbin from a piece of cereal-box cardboard, put a small slit at one end to hold the end of the yarn, and wind the waste yarn onto it. I save the cards of waste yarn for plastic canvas stitchery.

— *Audrey Krier, Pine Island, MN*

Sinkers

A sinker is a weight used on knitting machines and cord knitters to anchor the knitting and keep enough tension on the yarn so the stitches will form correctly, as shown in *Fig. 139*. Sinkers are sold as accessories with many knitting machines, but if you need additional weight, such as for working with bulky yarns that tend to catch on the

Fig. 139

Cord knitter with sinker weight

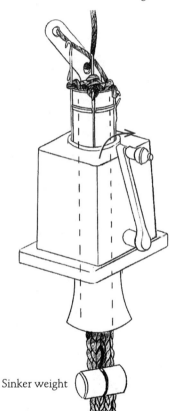

Sinker weight

Fig. 140

Decreasing

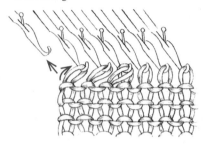

Increasing

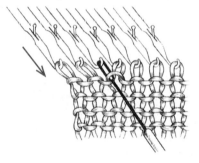

Fig. 141

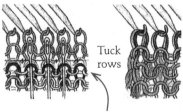

Tuck rows

Last row background loops

cord knitter, you can use almost anything to weight down the yarn. For example, an opened paper clip or metal hook attached on one end to the yarn and on the other to a sewing weight (for cutting out patterns), a kitchen implement, or a fishing weight (available in sporting goods stores in various sizes) makes a perfectly good yarn weight. The key is to add enough weight for the stitches to knit off smoothly, but not so much weight that it prevents the machine from operating freely.

INCREASES, DECREASES, AND TUCKS
Full-fashioned decreases and increases

Full-fashioned decreases create a smooth selvage. Move a stitch or group of stitches from the edge toward the center of the work, so that the needle at the point of decrease carries two stitches. Use a transfer tool to shift all the stitches outside the decrease at once, if possible (*Fig. 140*). Increases are similar, but to prevent a hole, lift a bar from the row below to fill the empty needle.

Tucks

To machine-knit a tuck, work twice as many rows as the desired width of the tuck in whatever pattern you desire. Use a one-, two-, or three-prong transfer tool to hang the last row of loops of the background yarn over the stitches on the final row of the tuck, as shown in *Fig. 141*. This will fold the tuck rows in half and cause a raised tuck to form on the right side of the work. Raise the tension one or two numbers to knit the next row in the background yarn. Then resume normal knitting tension.

MACHINE-KNITTING TECHNIQUES
Smocking on machine knits

I recently decided to use smocking to control the stretching I anticipated in a ribbed, drop-shoulder sweater I was machine-knitting. I set the tension tighter at each row I planned to smock so it was easy to see horizontal lines. The smocking went quickly, and the shoulders didn't sag.

—*D. Bird, Guemes Island, WA*

Striped knits and the NeedleMaster

I've found a strategy to produce honeycomb shapes for my scrap afghan. To make equilateral hexagons, I cast on 12 stitches and increase as per the pattern. When the stitches on the needle equal three times the number cast on (36), I decrease until I reach the number cast on. Then I bind off.

Also, using the Boye NeedleMaster™ kit made by Wrights®, I've found that when the coupler starts to wear, I can make a fresh start by snipping the ⅛ inch of worn plastic from each end. The loss in length will hardly be noticeable during the next several jaunts around the world with this versatile kit.

—*Thomas Walsh, Seattle, WA*

Isolation lace

I have a knitting machine that has a lace carriage but no isolation capabilities. Here's how I make isolation lace motifs anyway. I knit the garment in stockinette but don't assemble it. Then I shape and knit the lace pattern with my lace carriage. Using a fadeaway fabric marker, I trace the design on the garment where I want it. If I think

that extra support or a backing is necessary, I put a piece of nylon organdy on top of the outline. Using a serger or a zigzag stitch on my sewing machine, I sew around the tracing, covering the edges of the nylon organdy. Then I turn the piece over and carefully cut away only the stockinette stitches inside the stitching.

Finally, with the garment right-side up, I pin the lace design in place over the cutout or cutout and organdy, being sure to cover the serging stitches. When I use a straight stitch and sewing machine to attach the lace, I also edge it with purchased lace. For a completely knit look, I duplicate-stitch by hand around the lace, using the same yarn.

—*Ellen J. Riggan, Gloucester, VA*

BINDING OFF AND MANAGING YOUR ENDS
An alternative to tubular bind-off

I do most of my knitting on a standard-gauge knitting machine and work the ribbing by hand from the top down when the pieces are complete, using small (0 to 2) needles. It's

Fig. 142

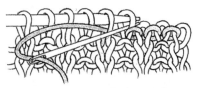

Insert tapestry needle from right to left and back to front in second stitch from point of knitting needle. Then go left to right and front to back in end stitch, and drop it.

hard to get a good tubular bind-off in a small gauge, but I've found that a technique of Elizabeth Zimmermann's gives a neat, elastic edge.

Hold the work on a single needle with the right side facing you. Break off the yarn, leaving a tail about four times the length of the piece to be bound off, and thread it on a tapestry needle. Bring the needle through the second loop from the end from right to left and back to front. Then insert the needle into the first stitch from left to right and front to back, and slip the first stitch off the needle, as shown in *Fig. 142*.

Repeat across with an even tension. When you get to the last pair of stitches, bring the needle through the top of the first stitch to the back of the work, and weave it in.

— *Patricia Tongue Edraos, Boston MA*

Machine-knitting with no loose ends

When I'm machine-knitting a design that requires color changing, I get rid of the cut ends by looping, or e-wrapping, them around several needles on the next two or three rows. This locks in the ends, which don't show on the right side and which can be clipped away.

— *Barbara Flett, Princeton, BC, Canada*

Managing yarn ends on the knitting machine

When introducing a new yarn at the end of a machine-knit row, instead of attaching the end to the stand after threading the carriage, take the end from under the carriage and manually knit the first stitch with it. Snip the new and old ends to 2 or 3 inches, and clip them together with a clothespin so they hang from the work and weight the new stitch. This saves yarn, the work is neater, and you don't have to remember to untie the ends from the stand later.

— *Enid Zucker, Southbury, CT*

SEAMS AND NECKLINES
Machine and hand knitters meet at the seams

I'm a machine knitter and have been using Rick Mondragon's hand-knitting method for joining seams by hanging a "turning thread" of a completed section on the machine every two rows as I knit a new section. For example, after knitting the front of a pants leg, I cast on for the back, then hang the first turning thread from the front leg on the last needle in work on the side opposite the carriage. I knit two rows so I'm again on the side opposite the hanging piece, and hang the next turning thread on the last needle. I can do this all the way up to join the inner and outer leg seams.

— *Anne Rogers, East Petersburg, PA*

From swatch to seam

I use the tension swatch yarn from machine knitting for hand work like weaving seams, crocheting necklines, and working sleeve edgings. I can take my knitting project with me to finish on vacation without taking extra yarn along.

— *Sharon Collins, Pocatello, ID*

Precise cut-and-sew necklines for machine knitters

Although I prefer to machine-knit fabric to shape, it is sometimes necessary or easier to use the cut-and-sew method at the neckline. This is especially true of double jacquard, many double-bed fabrics, and some patterning stitches such as tuck, slip, or a complex Fair Isle. I have discovered two methods of marking the seamline while knitting that ensure the neckline is cut precisely. I use these methods with an automatic patterning device, but they could also be used with a written pattern.

For double-jacquard fabrics, knit the pattern until the neckline shaping begins. Following the drawn or written pattern, transfer the stitches indicated for binding off from the ribber bed to the main bed. Place the ribber needles into nonworking position following the transfer. Continue knitting in pattern to the top of the garment, transferring stitches as necessary. It may be necessary to pull those needles holding transferred stitches to upper working or holding position before knitting every row so that they knit every time. The area transferred to the main bed knits in tiny stripes with stitches much smaller than the rest of the pattern, making it easy to see where the neckline is to be cut, as shown in the top drawing of *Fig. 143*. Cut about ¼ inch above the regular jacquard pattern. The tiny stitches in the cut area hold

Fig. 143

Double-Jacquard Fabric

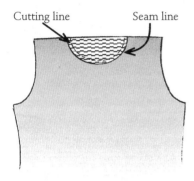

Cutting line   Seam line

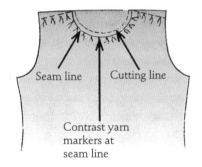

Seam line   Cutting line

Contrast yarn
markers at
seam line

together tightly, and there is little danger of unraveling with careful handling.

For other double-bed fabrics, the area being transferred becomes a single-bed fabric easily distinguishable from the main pattern. As a single-bed fabric, it is also more stable when being cut.

For single-bed fabrics, when neckline shaping is reached, lay short lengths of contrast yarn in the hooks of selected needles to mark the stitches that would normally be bound off. For the first bind-off, which may involve 10 to 20 stitches, mark the first, middle, and last stitches with the contrast yarn and, holding onto the contrast yarn as the carriage passes it, knit the row. Be careful not to pull the needles out of position when laying in the contrast yarn; doing so will cause the pattern to knit incorrectly. Continue knitting in pattern, marking the line of shaping every four to six rows. This will give a precise line to follow when cutting (see the bottom drawing of *Fig. 143*). Cut ¼ inch above the line. I leave the yarn markers attached while positioning the garment and neckband on the machine for linking together.

— *Peggy C. Durant, Clearfield, PA*

ODDS AND ENDS
Fixing punch-card errors

When punching new patterns for the knitting machine, I often make a mistake or decide to change a design after sampling. To cover a space that I punch incorrectly, I use white freezer tape. It's much better than clear tape because it gives the visual aid I need in punching.

— *Hannelore Ring, San Diego, CA*

Knit your own coil

You can make your own coil or rope with a knitting machine. Double-bed knitting machines can be set to knit circular tubes of various sizes by placing one of the beds out of work. If your machine is a single bed, you will have to move the cam box back to the right side after knitting the stitches right to left. Pass the yarn under the needles before beginning your next row of stitches. Knit the rope using a tight tension and a firm yarn. This knitted coil can be used to make baskets, rugs, or mats either by hand or sewing machine. The coil needs no core or fabric scraps.

— *Ellen Riggan, Gloucester, VA*

Drawing knitting-machine patterns

To draw accurate half-scale patterns for my knitting machine, I use a Macintosh® computer and Microspot MacDraft™. This software is used primarily for architectural drawing. With it you can draw smooth arcs for a neckline and can print to quarter and half scales.

After drawing the garment pattern, you can add original intarsia designs, place a single decorative motif wherever you like, etc. These design elements can be easily manipulated without disrupting the garment pattern, which can be reprinted with or without them.

— *Mary Louise Vidas, Mount Airy, NC*

Spinning to machine-knit

It is a faulty assumption that handspun yarns are too heavy and/or too irregular to use on a standard machine as is. Not so. I've been spinning for a number of years, and since I was taught to spin a single weighing 2,500 yards per pound, I've had no trouble putting that yarn, plied, on my knitting machine.

I use a double-bed Superba® and I regularly show and sell garments made from my own handspun knit on that machine. I spin all fibers to a grist that will work on the machine, although each fiber may require a slightly different spinning technique to achieve that grist. I encourage my students to take the time to learn to vary their techniques so they can design the appropriate yarn for the product and fabric construction they have in mind.

If the hand spinner takes the time to construct a yarn in the range of 900 to 5,600 yards per pound plied (equivalent to a 2/20 to 2/6 worsted count) and makes the twist even, he or she should have few problems knitting it on a standard-pitch machine.

— *Catherine Jacinta de la Cruz, Sebastopol, CA*

SEVEN

CROCHET TIPS

Stitches

Crochet Techniques

Multicolor Crocheting

Crochet
   Troubleshooting

Finishing Touches

Odds and Ends

STITCHES

Getting started

A slip knot and chain is the basis of all crochet. Make a slip knot by forming a loop and pulling the yarn from behind the loop through to the front with the crochet hook, as shown in the left-hand drawings of *Fig. 144;* tighten gently. Make a chain by wrapping the yarn over the hook (yo), and pulling the hook and yarn through the loop, as shown in the right-hand drawing of *Fig. 144;* tighten and repeat.

An alternative to the plain chain

Here's an attractive, sturdy, and more finished-looking alternative to an ordinary crocheted chain foundation. It's ideal when you won't be adding another edge to the crocheted piece. Start with a slip knot. While holding it loose, make one chain. Insert the hook in the slip knot again and draw the thread through so that there are two loops on the hook, as shown in *Fig. 145.* Draw the thread through both of them, then adjust the tension to even out the stitch you just made. *Pull slightly to get some slack on the loop

Fig. 144

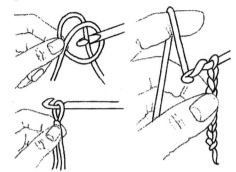

on the hook, then insert the hook in the loop closest to hook. Pull the thread through the two loops now on the hook. Repeat from *. This cord also makes a strong, good-looking button loop or belt loop. Leave a long tail at the beginning and at the end of the cord to sew into the seam allowance of the garment.
— *Gladys Shue, York, PA*

Single crochet

Single crochet (sc) is a two-step stitch that's relatively short in height and is useful for fitting a lot of detailed patterning into a small area; it makes a firm, nonstretchy fabric. Insert the hook from front to back through

Fig. 145

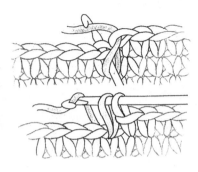

Fig. 146

both loops of the stitch below *(Fig. 146)*. Yarn over and pull up a loop; you now have two loops on the hook. Yarn over again and pull through both loops.

Square single crochet

Single crochet isn't a square stitch, which causes a problem in following graphed or charted designs. To make a square single crochet, put the hook through the completed row as usual, yarn over, and pull up a loop (two loops on the hook). Yarn over; work off one loop, leaving two loops on the hook; then yarn over and work off both loops *(Fig. 147)*. This really puts a chain stitch in the middle, adding just enough extra height to square the stitch.

— *Edith Frankel, Hannawa Falls, NY*

Fig. 147

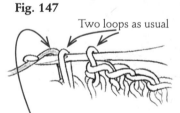
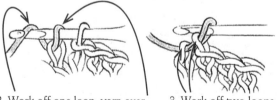

Two loops as usual

1. Pull up one loop, yarn over.   2. Work off one loop, yarn over.   3. Work off two loops.

Half double crochet

Half double crochet (hdc) is slightly taller than a single crochet. Yarn over and insert the hook into the work; yarn over and pull up a loop (see drawing A of *Fig. 148*). Yarn over and pull through all three loops on the hook (drawing B).

Fig. 148

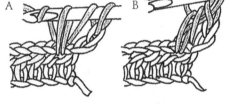

A   B

Double crochet

Double crochet (dc) results in a taller stitch that works up more quickly than single crochet. Yarn over, insert the hook through the loops as for single crochet, then yarn over and pull up a loop; you now have three

Fig. 149

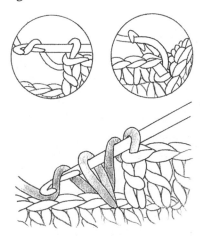

Crab-stitch crochet

Crab-stitch crochet, also called backward crochet, produces a beautiful corded edging. It's worked almost like single crochet, except from left to right. Work a row of single crochet from right to left, as usual. Do not turn the work. Chain one, *insert the hook under the next stitch to the right, pick up the yarn by dropping the head of the hook over it, and draw up a long loop *(Fig. 151)*. Wrap yarn over the hook and pull through both loops on the hook *(Fig. 152)*.* Repeat from * to *.

Fig. 151

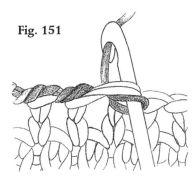

Fig. 152

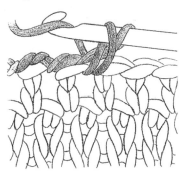

loops on the hook, as shown in *Fig. 149.* Yarn over and pull through two of the loops, then yarn over again and pull through the remaining two loops on the hook.

Treble crochet

Treble or triple crochet (tr) makes a tall stitch. Yarn over twice (see drawing A of *Fig. 150);* insert hook into work. Yarn over and pull up a loop; yarn over again and pull through first two loops only. Yarn over and pull through next two loops; yarn over and pull through last two loops on hook. (Drawing B shows the completed stitch.)

Fig. 150

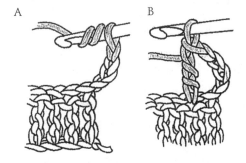

A   B

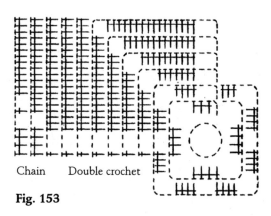

Chain   Double crochet

Fig. 153

Filet crochet

Filet crochet forms designs from square meshes of solid and open crochet. Each open mesh is made of three chain stitches separated by one double crochet, and four double crochets make the solid blocks. Directions for filet crochet are often given in charts similar to knitting charts. To read the chart *(Fig. 153),* right-handers begin in the bottom right-hand corner and read Row 1 to the left, then Row 2 to the right. Open squares in the chart represent meshes, while dots indicate solid blocks.

Fig. 154

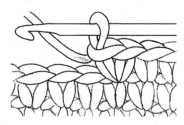

CROCHET TECHNIQUES

Increasing and decreasing

To increase (inc), crochet (single or double crochet) two stitches in one stitch, as shown in *Fig. 154.*

Working a decrease (dec) narrows crochet by eliminating a stitch. To decrease in single crochet, start by pulling up a loop as usual. Now insert the hook into the following stitch, yarn over, and pull up a loop (see the top drawing of *Fig. 155);* yarn over and pull yarn through all three loops on the hook. To decrease in double crochet, start by working a stitch as usual; stop at the last step when there are two loops left on the hook. Yarn over, insert the hook into the following stitch and pull up a loop, yarn over and pull through two loops, then yarn over and pull through the remaining three loops on the hook, as shown in the bottom drawing of *Fig. 155.*

Crocheting around a stitch

Crocheting around a stitch means inserting the hook through the crocheted fabric around the whole stem or post of a stitch. You can

Fig. 155 Decrease in Single Crochet

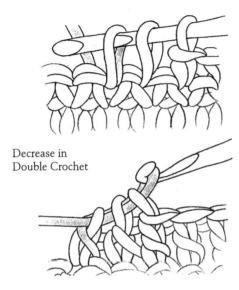

Decrease in
Double Crochet

Fig. 156

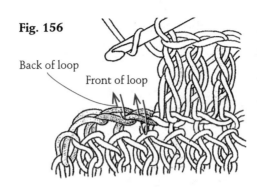

Back of loop

Front of loop

use this technique to attach a stitch to a previously worked area, and to create texture in the fabric by raising and lowering stitches.

Working into the front or back loop

Crochet is usually worked into both the front and back loops at the top of a stitch in the row below, with the hook inserted from front to back. When you insert the hook in the front loop (front of loop) only or back loop

(back of loop) only of the stitch, as shown in *Fig. 156,* the other loop remains on the fabric as a horizontal bar. This bar becomes part of the pattern or serves as a loop to be picked up and worked later.

Working around the post

Working around the front post *(Fig. 157)* means crocheting around the body, or post, of a stitch from the front side of the fabric, which causes the stitch to be raised above the surface.

Working around the back post is the same technique, except that it is worked from the back side of the fabric, as shown in *Fig. 157;* this causes the stitch to recede below the surface of the fabric.

Fig. 157

Working around a post

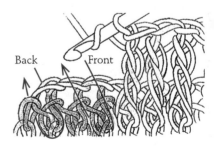

Back   Front

Fig. 158

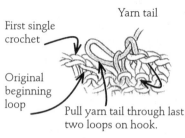

Yarn tail

First single crochet

Original beginning loop

Pull yarn tail through last two loops on hook.

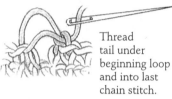

Thread tail under beginning loop and into last chain stitch.

Finish the V on the back and weave the tails into the work.

Perfect crochet joinery

Are you bothered by the not-so-perfect join at the beginning and end of a decorative, finishing round of single crochet? Try this invisible join: Begin the round by inserting the hook in the spot desired and pull a loop through. Do not chain, but work a single crochet in the next stitch and all around the piece. When you return to the beginning, work the last stitch loop as usual. Cut the yarn. Complete the last stitch by pulling the end through the two loops on the hook (Fig. 158). With a tapestry needle, thread the yarn end under the original beginning loop and back in the top of the last chain where the single crochet stitches ended. This new chain completes the first stitch of the round.

— *Susan Z. Douglas, Topsham, ME*

Crocheted buttonholes

Skip-and-chain buttonholes: Single crochet makes a good border or placket background for the *horizontal skip and chain*. When you reach the beginning of the buttonhole, place your button over the next stitches to see how many to skip. The height

of the row adds to the size of the hole, so, if your button is four stitches across, skip only three stitches, chaining instead, then continue with the row. Returning in the next row, single crochet in the chain stitches as usual.

With double crochet, this method can produce either round or vertical openings. A one- or two-stitch skip makes what looks like a vertical or round buttonhole. It won't hold a standard round button securely, but it works well with relatively large oval or toggle buttons. A larger skip makes a very large buttonhole because of the height of the stitch.

You can make the buttonhole smaller by working slip stitches or single crochet inside the perimeter for a *bound buttonhole*. Bind the hole right after you complete it, without cutting the yarn, so there are no loose ends. Don't bind around the entire bar of the double-crochet stitches on the edges. Insert the hook through only two threads at a time so the stitch won't be pulled away from its neighbor.

You can also use the one-stitch skip-and-chain to make *invisible buttonholes* on a mock rib worked in double crochet. To do this, with the right side facing, chain one where you would normally work a rear bar stitch. Finish the row. On the return, work a standard double crochet in chain stitch (because there's no bar to insert the hook around). Work the bar stitches on the third row; the buttonhole will retreat to the back of the fabric.

For a garment made in brighter colors or with a hipper design, I prefer a *skip-and-chain in sweater stitch.* In the row before the buttonhole, single crochet where the hole will be formed. Skip and chain in the next row as usual. In the third row, work single crochet along the chain stitches. Return to the pattern stitch thereafter.

For a *vertical buttonhole,* pretend that the start of the buttonhole is the end of the row. Work back and forth on this side of the hole an odd number of rows. If you plan to skip stitches, chain or make foundation stitches for the width of the hole. Then knot the yarn and carry it loosely to the beginning point on the other side of the hole. Enclose the carried yarn in turning stitches as you work the same number of rows back and forth. Work the next row across. When you get to the knot, insert the hook in the last two loops of the stitch as if you hadn't finished it before. This covers the knot smoothly.

Loop buttonholes: Button loops are generally part of a finishing row worked along the edge of the garment. The finishing will look nicer if you work at least two rows. Work a regular pattern along the raw edge for the first row to create a smooth outer edge. Sweater stitch is good because the row is short and it doesn't call much attention to itself. Make your loops on the second row. They can end in the stitch they began in, in the next stitch, or a few stitches away, or they can be stretched all the way out to look like horizontal skip-and-chain buttonholes

For an *N-treble loop,* yarn over about five times or so. Insert the hook in the stitch where the loop will end, yarn over, and pull through the stitch. Continue to yarn over and pull through two loops at a time until one loop remains on the hook.

For a *twist loop,* elongate the original loop to two or three times the length of the planned loop. With the hook inserted, twist the loop until it twists back on itself when folded in half. Then insert the hook through the base at the twist at the starting point and slip stitch to secure it to the row. Stitch to where you want to join the twist to the edge, insert the hook through the end of the twist,

Fig. 159

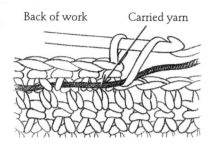

Back of work   Carried yarn

Fig. 160

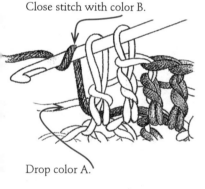

Close stitch with color B.

Drop color A.

and enclose it in the next stitch.

For a *covered chain loop,* chain to the desired length and join to the start. Work single crochet over the chain loop to improve its appearance and strengthen it.

An *enclosed loop* is a placket constructed around evenly spaced loops, a technique I developed. As you work the edging, when you reach a loop, decrease in the row and work a layer of slip stitches over the loop. After three or four rows, the edge will be even and the loops will be covered. Work a few more rows to complete the placket.

— *Mary Rhodes McGoveran, Boulder Creek, CA*

MULTICOLOR CROCHETING
Carrying a second color

To carry a second yarn color across a row, hold it at the back of the work and catch it in every three to four stitches by twisting it around the main yarn and crocheting around it, as shown in *Fig. 159.* Only the main color is visible from the front.

To change colors in crochet, work in color A until two loops of the last stitch in that color remain on the hook, then use color B to close the stitch *(Fig. 160).*

Crocheting a reversible afghan

Work in single crochet with a large hook, such as size K, with worsted-weight yarn; this will produce a thick, lofty fabric. At the end of each row, break the yarn (leaving a 5-inch end) and turn the work. Alternate two yarn colors, one for each side of the afghan.

Here's how the pattern works: First make a chain the desired length (the width of the afghan) and break the yarn. For the first row, single crochet only into the front loop of the chain. On the second row, insert the hook into the remaining (back) loop of the chain and the front loop of the first row and crochet the loops together. Repeat the second row throughout, inserting the hook into the remaining loop of the row below and the front loop of the most recent row, and alternate colors to produce a two-sided fabric.

After crocheting the afghan to the desired length, you can knot the yarn ends (four ends per overhand knot) to form fringe along the sides.

— *Karen Morris*

CROCHET TROUBLESHOOTING

Untwisted crochet turning chains

If you find it difficult to enter your turning chain from the previous crocheted row to pick up a stitch, you may have twisted it in turning your work. To avoid this, always turn the piece away from your body, counterclockwise for right-handers and clockwise for lefties.

— *Gladys Shue, York, PA*

Correcting uneven crochet edges

To eliminate the undesirable holes and gaps that sometimes occur at the end of a row of double crochet, a correction is often made in the space after the turning chain. But I was not pleased with this result and discovered that changing the length of the turning chain from three to two stitches reduces the slack. Chain two and turn counterclockwise for a cleaner edge.

— *Gladys Shue, York, PA*

How to attain drapier crochet

The crochet-sweater-that-looks-like-an-afghan problem is common among crocheters who use worsted-weight yarn at a gauge of 3 stitches per inch. To solve this problem, use a lighter, sport-weight yarn at a firm gauge (at least 5 to 7 stitches per inch). To create relief designs, use a background of double crochet. You'll get the texture you want without a lot of excess bulk.

— *Mary Rhodes McGoveran, Boulder Creek, CA*

FINISHING TOUCHES

Crocheted edgings on wovens

Attaching crocheted edges to firmly woven materials can be difficult if the yarn is too bulky to be drawn easily through the material. I use cotton embroidery floss to make a row of chain stitches about a seam's width from the edge of the material. I can then attach crocheted strips or shapes by single-crocheting them to the chain loops, or I can crochet an edging by working directly from the chained line. When they match the

Fig. 161

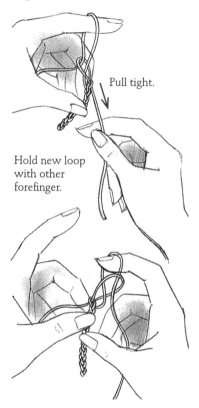

Pull tight.

Hold new loop with other forefinger.

156

color of the edging, the cotton stitches are virtually invisible.

— *Elizabeth Meineke, Prescott, AZ*

Crochet a ruffle

To make a ruffle at the cuff of a glove, increase in every other stitch or every stitch in the first row to make the ruffle as full as you want; experiment on a swatch.

Crochet a waistband

Here's a great way to crochet a sweater waistband with the "elastic" stretch of a knit. Using a fine yarn or floss that gives about 8 single-crochet stitches to the inch, ch 26 sts with a No. 3 steel crochet hook. Sc in 2nd chain from hook and in each ch across (25 sc). This row of 25 sc is your foundation chain. Ch 1, turn each row. Sc in back lp of each sc across. Repeat last row until piece, when slightly stretched, measures 30 inches (for sizes 10 to 12) or desired waist measurement. Don't cut the thread when you finish; you'll use it to join the ends of the waistband to make a circle.

Next row: Sl st together back lp of first sc (the first sc on the last row of the waistband) and first st of the foundation chain, *sl st together back lp of next sc and next st in ch*, repeat from * to * across. End off. Sew the waistband to the lower edge of the sweater, easing the sweater to fit.

— *Marilyn J. Panter, Walnut Creek, CA*

Making a round cord

Here's a quick way to crochet a round and even cord of any length or thickness, using no hook, only your hands.

For a small cord, start with yarn at least six times the length you want the finished cord to be. Fold the yarn in half and make a slip loop. Working with both forefingers, alternately pull the yarn through the loop, first from one side and then from the other (see the top drawing of *Fig. 161*). Slip the loop alternately from the holding finger to the other forefinger as it makes the new loop, pulling down on the cord as it forms (see the bottom drawing of *Fig. 161*). You'll find the motion is easy once you get it. When you reach the desired length, pull the loose ends through the loop and weave them into the cord.

For a thick cord, start with multiple strands of yarn—double, triple, etc. There are endless uses for a cord like this—ties for hats, booties, sweaters, plant hangers, even shoelaces. I've made sneaker laces using two school colors of fine acrylic or nylon yarn. A tight wrap of Scotch® tape, wax, or glue will shape the tips.

— *Jean Leavitt, Newtown, CT*

ODDS AND ENDS
Pain-free crochet

Hours of working with a crochet hook take a toll on my hands and wrists, so I've experimented with padding the hook handles. A bigger grip is helpful, but tape and padding seem to slip off eventually. When my husband changed the gas lines in his car a while back, he had several feet of clear rubber tubing left over, so I tried slipping the tubing over the handle of my crochet hook, and it worked beautifully. The hose slides onto the smaller hooks easily, gripping the handle without slipping. (You'll have to pad the smallest hooks with masking tape first, though.) For larger sizes, dipping the hook

into hand lotion makes insertion easier. If the handle still seems too narrow, larger-diameter rubber hoses are available. Gas-line hose can be found at any auto parts store. A foot of hose will cover three or four handles with a comfortable, nonslip grip. Best of all, my hands no longer ball into fists while I sleep.

— *Suzanne Deal-Fitzgerald, Monticello, GA*

Handmade crochet hooks

Ten years ago, my husband bought me two handmade wooden crochet hooks for Christmas. Since I was afraid that they'd break or that the fancy decorations on the ends would chip off, I didn't use either one until recently. Besides, I thought that they were too fancy to be functional. I was wrong on all counts. The special features of a handmade wooden hook *(Fig. 162)* are the lump in the handle, the beads at the end, and the style of the taper. The lump and the beads are both handy when you want to put your work down for a while. If you poke the wooden hook through the fabric in two places with the lump in the middle, the hook stays put. Slide the working loop onto

Fig. 162

Beads

Lump

Put hook twice through work with lump in middle to hold it; use beads to secure loop.

the bead section near the end of the hook. Tighten it, and it will stay there.

I thought that the absence of a thumb rest would be a problem in controlling tension. It would be for fine thread, but for worsted- or sport-weight wool, it doesn't make a difference. I also thought that the variable taper would cause stitch inconsistencies, but it doesn't.

— *Mary Rhodes McGoveran, Boulder Creek, CA*

Crochet counting aids

I usually crochet with a tray table in front of me, and I count rows or stitches by moving whatever is on the table—pencils, paper clips, spoons, a coffee cup. I build a pile and then "unbuild" the pile. Moving a small item is faster than picking up a pen and writing after each row.

— *Nancy Kelly, Brooksville, FL*

Working at the speed of crochet

There seems to be a myth that crochet is, or should be, faster than knitting, and a gauge of 6 stitches per inch is considered acceptable for knitting but intolerable for crochet.

This really doesn't make sense. There is no tall stitch in knitting comparable to a double crochet, and even in single crochet there will always be fewer rows per inch than if the piece were knit. Therefore, that it takes longer to crochet a row of stitches than to knit the same number of stitches is balanced by the need for fewer rows.

— *Linda S. Sang, Rosemead, CA*

Understanding crocheted fabric

Crocheting and knitting seem to have a lot in common, but there are basic differences between the two fabric structures. In knit fabric, the threads pass over, under, and around one another to build the fabric but are not locked in place. The fabric is flexible because of the stretch of the yarn and because each stitch can shift position in relation to the neighboring stitches. In crocheted fabric, each stitch is like a knot. The fabric is flexible mainly because of the yarn's stretch. Individual stitches have some give, but once this give has been stretched out, it cannot be restored.

When you look at knit fabric, you are aware of the fabric as a whole. When you look at crocheted fabric, you are aware of the individual stitches. Crochet stitches are also thicker than knit stitches, so crocheted fabric is thicker than knit fabric in the same yarn.

Rumors persist that crochet should always be worked loosely. This rule may be appropriate for a decorative fabric that won't be pulled, hung, or stretched in use, but garments are different. Crocheted fabric for a sweater shouldn't be too tight or dense, but loose stitches result in a droopy garment in no time, and they'll also snag on things more easily.

The integrity of the crocheted stitches—the degree to which they hold their shape—depends on the hook you choose for the yarn. A general rule is to use the smallest hook that's comfortable for the yarn. If it's too large, the fabric and stitches will quickly stretch out of shape, but if it's too small, it will split the yarn.

When thinking about hook size, consider also the spaces between stitches. Crocheted stitches are larger than knit ones, so the spaces in a crocheted fabric are bigger—big enough to reduce the warmth of the garment. Using the smallest hook that works comfortably with the yarn reduces the size of these spaces and minimizes their effect.

Since crocheted fabric is thicker than knit fabric, a sweater crocheted with sport-weight yarn can be as warm and heavy as one knit with worsted-weight yarn. And if you use a worsted-weight yarn to copy in crochet a sweater knit in worsted-weight yarn, the crocheted fabric will be too thick and heavy.

— *Mary Rhodes McGoveran, Boulder Creek, CA*

Recommended Hook and Yarn Sizes

Yarn	Hook	Sts/in.	Rows/in. (gauge in double crochet)	Garment season
Fingering	4–2 steel	6–8	4	Spring, summer
Sport	00 steel–F	4–6	3	Fall, winter
Worsted	F–G	4	2	Winter (sweaters) Fall (jackets)
Lopi	I	3	2	Winter (jackets)

EIGHT

FINISHING AND CARING FOR YOUR PROJECT

Seams

Sewing in Ends, Edging, and Fringe

Blocking

Shoulder Pads

Personalizing Your Work

Washing Wool and Handknits

Repairing Handknits

Odds and Ends

SEAMS

Don't bother with selvages

Selvages have more often ruined knitted articles than they have enhanced them. Why do something different with the edge stitches of knitted fabric at all? The answer is that without special attention they often appear sloppy and ragged, but making contrived selvages of different stitches is not necessarily the best solution. It is generally better to make it a habit to tighten the edge stitches of all knitting as follows: Work the first stitch of a row in the usual way. Insert the needle to make the second stitch. Stop. Firmly pull on the yarn to tighten the previous stitch. Complete the second stitch as usual. This way, sloppy and ragged edges will simply not happen.

The answer to the question "When to make a selvage?" is never, if the edge will be part of a border or will be finished off by crocheting, picking up stitches, or weaving a seam. It is exceedingly difficult to make a smooth, even crocheted edging over a vertical edge where the initial stitch has been slipped, as in chain, French, or English selvages. It will often be necessary to make two single-crochet stitches in one slipped stitch, which will cause an unsightly hole. Where the two edge stitches have been worked in a different pattern stitch, there will be a valley or a ridge next to the crocheted edge. The same will be true when you're picking up stitches along vertical edges. When you're weaving seams, any slipped or garter-stitch selvage will have a different row gauge from that of the adjacent fabric, and the seam will tend to be shorter, causing it to pucker. Hiding the selvage within the seam will add unnecessary bulk.

When the edge stitches will be part of a knitted-in-one-piece border, such as the edge of an afghan or the front bands of a cardigan, a two-stitch selvage alone will be insufficient to keep the fabric from rolling to the back. At least four stitches of a knitted-in-one-piece border are necessary to prevent curling.
— *Maggie Righetti*

Knitting a seam

Knitting a seam, also called joinery bind-off, is a method of binding off and joining two edges of open stitches at the same time, which results in a flat, flexible seam and eliminates the need for sewing. The joinery bind-off

Fig. 163

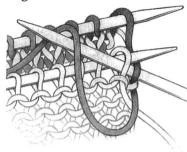

Fig. 163-A

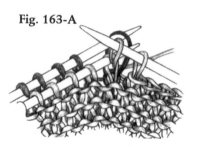

works well for finishing vertical seams, such as side and center-back seams, on garments that are knitted sideways.

To knit and bind off two edges together, place the two fabrics right sides together with the open stitches of each edge on a needle pointing to the right *(Fig. 163)*. Insert a third needle purlwise into the first stitch on the back needle, then the first stitch on the front needle, as shown; purl the two stitches together. (Alternatively, you can knit the two stitches together, entering the stitch on the front needle first, but many knitters find that purling is easier to maneuver.) Repeat for the next pair of stitches. There are now two stitches on the right needle; pass the first stitch over the second stitch to cast off. Repeat across the row.

You can also use this bind-off method to form a decorative ridge on the right side by placing the two fabrics wrong sides together, then casting off as described above.

Bind off and join pieces in one step

You can knit the back and front pieces together to bind off and join them in one step. Be sure the front and back shoulders

have the same number of stitches on the bind-off row. Put matching front and back shoulders on two needles so both points are at the neck or armhole edge. You can hold them right sides together and work from the wrong side to create an invisible join, or hold them wrong sides together (working from the right side) to make a decorative ridge on the right side.

Insert a third needle into the first stitch on the front and the first stitch on the back as if they were a single stitch. Knit as shown in *Fig. 163-A;* repeat. Bind off whenever there are two stitches on the right needle by passing the first stitch over the second.

Six seams for sweaters

There are three stitches that go a long way toward finishing sweaters: the slip-stitch crochet, backstitch, and mattress stitch. Using those stitches, here are six basic seams for knit sweaters *(see Fig. 164–169)*.
— *Susan Guagliumi*

Decorative seaming

Knitting a three-stitch cord and joining a seam at the same time is an easy and

Fig. 164

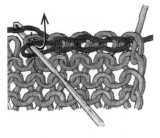

1. Slip-Stitch Crochet for Shoulder Seams

With right sides of fabric together and wrong side facing you, insert crochet hook through 1st stitch and pull loop of yarn through. With loop on w through stitch and through loop on hook so one loop remains on hook. Continue. ("Live" stitches are shown. The stitch holder has been deleted for clarity. For a bound-off edge, the seam would be done in the row below the bind-off.)

Fig. 165

2. Slip-Stitch Crochet for Side Seams

With right sides together, work one full stitch from edge into every other bar.

Fig. 167

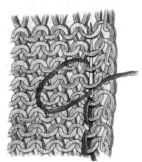

4. Backstitch for Side Seams

With right sides together, work into every other space.

Fig. 166

3. Backstitch for Shoulder Seams

With right sides of fabric together and wrong side facing you, insert tapestry needle down into 1st stitch and up through 2nd stitch. Now go back down into 1st stitch, up through 3rd stitch, down into 2nd stitch, up through 4th stitch, down into 3rd stitch, up into 5th stitch. Continue. ("Live" stitches are shown. The stitch holder has been deleted for clarity.)

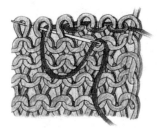

Fig. 168

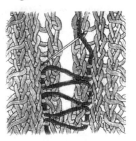

Fig. 169

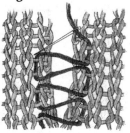

5 and 6. Mattress Stitch for Raglan Sleeves and Side Seams

Work with garment pieces side by side, right sides facing you. Work one full stitch from edge. Insert needle under two bars and back out on right-hand fabric, then under two bars and back out on left-hand fabric. Continue, the needle always entering a hole it previously exited. After every 6 stitches, pull firmly on yarn to bring the two edges together.

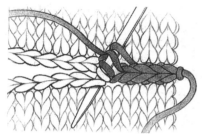

Fig. 170

Fig. 171

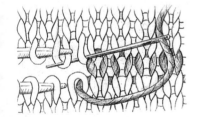

Fig. 172

attractive way to accomplish two tasks at once. Besides completing the seam, this technique adds a decorative garment detail in a matching or contrasting yarn.

Begin with the right sides of the garment pieces facing upward, butting together the edges that you want to join. Using double-pointed needles, cast on three stitches, then slide the left end of the same needle through the inner half of the bind-off chain or selvage stitch on each piece, as shown in *Fig. 170*. Next, knit the first two stitches. Insert the needle through the third stitch (the last stitch of the cord) and the two edge stitches and knit them all together, as shown in *Fig. 171*.

Repeat. For a selvage edge, work 8 to 10 consecutive stitches, then skip one stitch to give the correct tension between the knitted edge and the cord.

Grafting

Grafting, or Kitchener stitch, is used to join two open rows of knit stitches with a third row to create an invisible seam. You can join flat fabric held on needles, as shown in *Fig. 172*, or the live stitches from two ends of knitted cord. In each case, go into each stitch twice, using a tapestry needle threaded with yarn that is about four times the length of the seam. For a smooth look, it's important to match the weaving tension to the knitted stitches. When joining stitches on needles, after you have entered a stitch for the second time, drop it from its needle.

Kitchener stitches

When I first learned to do the Kitchener stitch, my teacher gave me a mantra to say to help remember where I was in the process. Holding the two needles of stitches parallel to each other, wrong sides together, yarn threaded through embroidery needle, begin with the first stitch on the front needle and say: "As if to knit and take it off," then the second stitch: "As if to purl and leave it on." Then do two stitches from the back needles: "As if to purl and take it off," then: "As if to knit and leave it on." Repeat two stitches from the front, two from the back, and so on. If you make a mistake in direction, you'll see it right away.

—*Sally Campbell, Cold Spring Harbor, NY*

Visible grafting edge

When grafting together seams on darker-colored sweaters, I find it difficult to see the individual edge stitches. To increase the visibility of the stitches and facilitate seaming, I knit all the edges to be joined with a lighter-colored yarn. Be careful to conceal the light-colored edge when you graft the seams together.

— *Susan M. Johnson, Ann Arbor, MI*

Vertical knit grafting

Have trouble grafting two pieces of knitting vertically? Here's a way to graft two stockinette pieces that makes the seam invisible and, with lighter-weight yarns, cannot be felt: Take a long strand of yarn and, starting at the top of the pieces on the stockinette side, join the edges with yarn lengths equal to that of one dropped stitch *(Fig. 173)*. (The yarn of one dropped stitch should be about four times the width of one knitted stitch.) When you have done the entire seam, take a crochet hook with a shank the same diameter as your knitting needle and, working from bottom to top, start picking up that "dropped" stitch. The last stitch on your hook will have to be woven in or fastened off.

— *Betty Salpekar, Pittsford, NY*

Reinforcing grafted shoulder seams

A shoulder seam that hasn't been bound off and is grafted to give a seamless look can stretch, allowing the sleeve to become longer. You can reinforce the graft without affecting its appearance by crocheting a chain along the inside of the shoulder seam, from neck to sleeve. Pick up the inside loop of every stitch or every other stitch. The final crochet stitch should go into the top of the sleeve. This will keep the shoulder from stretching and will help support the weight of the sleeve.

— *Dorothy Bird, Guemes Island, WA*

Grafting toes

I have recently braved knitting socks for the first time. Although it all went fairly smoothly, I found grafting the toe to be somewhat delicate an operation. To that

Fig. 173

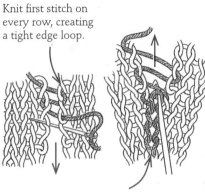

Knit first stitch on every row, creating a tight edge loop.

Build bridge through loops.

end, I have found it helpful to insert a shampoo bottle (any flat-topped container about 2 inches wide would do) into the sock to provide a small table upon which the remaining stitches can be grafted. The bottle itself goes between my knees, thus raising the sock to the perfect height and allowing me to hold it firmly without using my hands.
—*Stacey Callahan, Toulouse, France*

Seaming with slip-stitch crochet

Slip-stitch crochet produces a firm, even seam for joining two pieces of knitting. If possible, use yarn about half the weight of the project yarn in the same color so the seam won't be too bulky and it won't show. Place the pieces right sides together and *insert the hook through both pieces between the selvage or edge stitch and the next stitch, as

Fig. 174

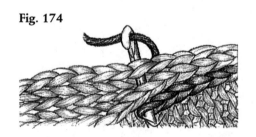

shown in *Fig. 174*. Catch the yarn and draw through a loop*. Repeat from * to * and draw the second loop through first loop; one loop remains. Continue drawing the second loop through the first loop to the end of the seam. To keep the seam flexible, be sure not to work too tightly.

Mattress stitch

Mattress stitch is a strong, nearly invisible method of seaming two pieces of knitting. It's worked from the right side, ideally with a long end of yarn left over from the initial cast-on. Join the lower edges by stitching back and forth between them in a figure-eight twice to form a firm, even base with no jog. Then begin mattress stitching: catch two horizontal bars just inside the edge stitch and carry the thread across to the other side, stitching under the next pair of bars, as shown in drawing A of *Fig. 175*. Snug up the thread every two or three stitches to pull the two pieces together without strain. A similar technique will also work for joining two bound-off edges. The "bars" are the stitches just before the bind-off chain, as shown in drawing B of *Fig. 175*.

Fig. 175 Mattress-stitch seam on stockinette

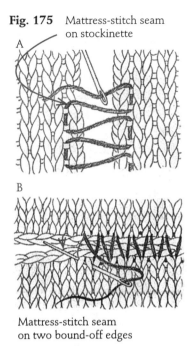

Mattress-stitch seam
on two bound-off edges

varying the selvages. For a knit one, purl one rib, put two knit stitches on each edge of the front, the back, and the cuffs. Mattress-stitch into the center of the second stitch from each edge. The result is what looks like a knit stitch at the join. The extra half-knit stitch on the seam rolls down slightly and produces a neater seam than you would get by grafting a knit stitch to a purl stitch, where the knit stitch always seems to roll over onto the purl stitch.

For a knit two, purl two rib, edge both sides of one piece with two knit stitches, and edge both sides of the other piece with three knit stitches. Or put two knit stitches on one edge and three knit stitches on the other edge of each piece, making sure that you will be joining a three-stitch edge to a two-stitch edge. Again, mattress-stitch through the center of the second stitch from each edge.

The best joining method of all is totally invisible because there is no join. Even when you knit a sweater in separate, flat pieces, you can make a perfect ribbing by knitting it on circular needles after you join the side seams of the sweater with mattress stitch. Begin the pieces above the rib with an invisible cast-on. After you have assembled

Fig. 176

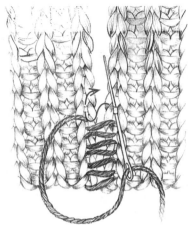

Mattress-stitch seam
on ribbing

On ribbed fabric, catch the end stitch on each piece to be joined in the center and sew across to the opposite stitch *(Fig. 176)*.

Joining ribbing

After several years of seeking the perfect rib, I have developed various techniques for joining ribbing. One of my favorites is

Fig. 177

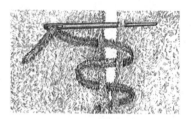

the garment, pick up the bottom stitches on a circular needle, making sure that you catch each selvage stitch after the second stitch from the edge. When you come around to the selvage stitch on each side, knit or purl it together with the stitch next to, and overlapping, it. You can do cuffs the same way with double-pointed needles.
— *Patricia Tongue Edraos, Boston, MA*

Baseball stitch

Use baseball stitch to sew two pieces of knitting together without a bulky seam. Leave a long cast-on tail on one piece to use for sewing. Thread the yarn onto a blunt tapestry needle and butt the two edges to be joined right sides up. Bring the needle up from the wrong side through the edge loop of the unattached piece, then across to the first piece and up through its next edge loop from its wrong side *(Fig. 177)*

Two straight pins hold knitting best

If I have to pin-baste my knitted garment together while I finish it, I use pairs of straight pins instead of one. Whether they end up parallel or crossed doesn't matter. While one pin may fall out easily, two pins lock each other in place. They do not move, even when I manipulate the knitted pieces.
— *Kristina Deimel, Bearsville, NY*

Basic assembly method for three sweaters

Round neck, set-in sleeves: Don't knot the beginning or ending yarn tails. If you left enough tail at the beginning of knitting, use it to start the seam and, when it runs out, start another piece of yarn, leaving at least a 5-inch tail to weave in later. With right sides together, pin and complete one shoulder seam using either slip-stitch crochet or backstitch. Either will produce a seam firm enough to support the sleeve without stretching. I prefer slip-stitch crochet off live stitches held on waste knitting but others find backstitch easier when working off a stitch holder. Just don't use single crochet—it's too bulky.

For machine knitters and hand knitters who prefer to work ribbing back and forth on straight needles, this is the time to knit the neckband. If front or back neckline stitches are on stitch holders, replace them on needles. You'll probably have to "make" some stitches along the vertical selvage edges of the front neckline. To do this, pick up (or hang, on the machine) stitches in those areas so you end up with the required number of stitches on the needles. If you bound off the neck stitches, pick up all the neck-edge stitches. Knit the neckband.

Complete the second shoulder seam the same way as the first. Work toward the neck and join the ends of the neckband as well. Hand knitters who prefer to knit the neckband on circular needles should do so after completing both shoulder seams and before adding the weight of the sleeves.

Once the shoulder seams and neckband are complete, you can proceed in either of two ways. Some knitters prefer to complete the side seams first, then set in the sleeves. But it's easier for beginners to join the sleeve cap to the body, then complete the side seams. Pin the sleeve cap to the armhole, right sides together, and either backstitch or slip-stitch crochet the seam, always working one stitch from the edge. Repeat for the second sleeve.

Construct the underarm and side seams, using slip-stitch crochet, backstitch, or mattress stitch. Mattress stitch is easiest to work on knit stitches with the right sides facing you. The other two methods are better for purl or texture stitches. Don't work a continuous seam. Rather, make one seam from hip to armhole, then a second seam from cuff to armhole, so any discrepancies can be eased invisibly.

Raglans: Raglan finishing is basically the same as finishing for a set-in sleeve, except there are three raglan-shoulder seams to make before the neckband is knit. The mattress stitch is wonderful for the full-fashioned edges of raglan seams. Work it with the right sides facing. Leave one back seam open and complete it after knitting the neckband if you're working on straight needles or on the machine. Close all four seams if you knit a circular band.

Cardigans: For cardigans, complete all seams first. Then make the front bands. These can be crocheted, knit horizontally off the front edges, or knit as separate vertical bands, which are then backstitched, slip-stitch-crocheted (fastest method), or mattress-stitched (neatest method) to the front edges.

Most patterns recommend a method. If you make separate bands, knit them to the given center-front measurement of the finished sweater. Don't measure the front edges, because they usually will have stretched a bit. Knit or crochet buttonholes as you knit the band, or machine-stitch them later. Always try a swatch first. After you've completed the front bands, pick up the neckline stitches, making stitches as necessary, and knit the neckband.

— *Susan Guagliumi*

Machine-sewing on knitting

When machine-stitching the armholes of my circular sweaters before cutting the center stitch for the opening, I used to have problems with the yarn catching in the feed dogs. I solved the problem by pinning a used fabric-softener sheet on the wrong side of the sweater, directly below the area to be stitched. The sheet tears away easily after I've stitched down both sides of the armhole.

— *Susan Terry, Norfolk, VA*

SEWING IN ENDS, EDGING, AND FRINGE

Helping hands work inside small knit items

When sewing in the tail ends, stitching a duplicate stitch, or sewing a reinforcement seam in a small, tubular knit item, such as a child's mitten, I find it very helpful to use a darning egg to keep the two layers of fabric separate and to help spread the fabric without overstretching it. The handle of the egg can also slip into a thumb or glove finger quite nicely.

— *Ann Prochowicz, Trempealeau, WI*

Crocheted edge finish

Make a nonrolling finish on your knits using single crochet and slip stitch on bound-off edges. With the right side of the garment facing you, draw up one loop under the first bind-off chain with a crochet hook, using either matching or contrasting yarn. To make a chain, wrap the yarn over the hook and pull the yarn through the loop on the hook (*Fig. 78*, step 1). Make one more chain, then draw up one loop through the second bind-off chain (two loops on hook). Yarn over, draw through both loops (*Fig. 178, step 2,* one single crochet made).

On the sweater bottom, single crochet across, chain one, and turn. Then, from the wrong side, slip-stitch under both loops of each single crochet (bottom drawing of *Fig. 178*). For circular hems like sleeves, single crochet around and join last stitch to first stitch with a slip stitch. Chain one, turn, and work the slip stitch from inside the sleeve.

Adding fringe

Fringe adds an attractive finish at the edges of a rug, and it's an easy detail to do. First, decide on the desired length for the fringe. Wrap yarn around a piece of cardboard cut to that size plus ½ inch for tying; you could also use an object that's the right size, such as a book or box. Cut the yarn along one side of the cardboard to create separate double-length strands. With a crochet hook, pull a group of two to three strands from back to front through the first hole on one end of the rug (as shown in *Fig. 179),* even the ends, and then tie them in a square knot close to the rug. Repeat for each hole across the width.

Trim the ends evenly, if necessary. For a variegated effect, you can combine different colors from the rug to make the fringe.

Grooming fringe

A wide-toothed plastic comb, sometimes called a pick or a hair-lift, works nicely to align all the strands when I'm pressing and trimming the fringe on knitted and crocheted shawls. I have purchased a few combs with different tooth widths for working with a variety of fringes.

— *Lois Manton, Montreal, PQ, Canada*

Fig. 178

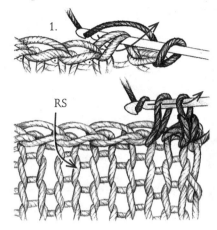
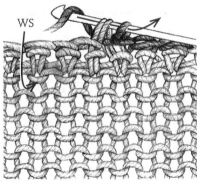

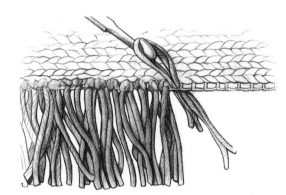

Fig. 179

BLOCKING

Blocking mixed-yarn sweaters

Combining yarns with different fiber contents produces interesting knitted effects and uses up leftover yarns, but the finished product can be difficult to block. Here's how I smooth the lumps and bumps in a multiyarn sweater: Thoroughly wet a large towel. Wring out the excess water and place the towel on a clean, flat surface (the top of a dryer works well). Carefully block and pin your sweater to half of the wet towel. Fold the other half over the sweater to form a sandwich and leave it for half a day. Uncover the sweater and leave it pinned to the towel overnight. In the morning, completely remove the towel and let your sweater dry flat. All those bumps and lumps should disappear.

— *Veronica Schmerling, Pittsburgh, PA*

Unusual surfaces aid knitters

A wonderful surface for blocking knits is a new carpet remnant that has a canvas backing. Turn it upside down and lay brown paper or cloth over the canvas to make a smooth, clean surface. The canvas is stiff, allows pins to go through easily, and holds the pins in place.

— *Susan Terry, Orlando, FL*

Using cork to steam

Using a small handheld steamer to fluff knits and flatten seams can be difficult because the steamer needs to be held upright to work properly. Instead, lay your knit garment on an old cork bulletin board and lean the board against a wall. The wool fibers stick to the pebbled surface so the sweater stays in place. This also makes it easy to reposition the sweater to steam all the surface areas.

— *Deborah Newton, Providence, RI*

Pizza-pan tam stretchers

A pizza pan from your local housewares store makes a great stretcher for knit tams. The pan is unbreakable, lightweight, and inexpensive, and it comes in many sizes including 12 and 14 inches.

— *Suzanne Correira, Austin, TX*

SHOULDER PADS
Knitted shoulder pads

Knitted shoulder pads can add shape and definition to a knitted garment, such as a sideways-knitted sweater. Ready-made, sewn shoulder pads of foam or batting can be too stiff for a soft sweater, but knitted shoulder pads define the shoulder while remaining flexible. And they're quick and easy to make, since they're basically a simple square of knitting folded diagonally in half.

To make a pad, knit a square 5 to 6 inches wide, using garter stitch (knit every row) for thickness. Fold the square in half and overcast the edges together using the yarn end, as shown in *Fig. 180*. Try on the garment and place the pad at the shoulder with the long, pointed side facing toward the neck and the folded edge along the edge of the shoulder line. Pin the pad in place, then tack it to the sweater with loose stitches at each corner. For thicker pads, use larger needles and a thick, lofty yarn, such as chenille.

Velcro for shoulder pads

I have a number of handknit sweaters that improved in appearance with the use of shoulder pads. I thought that foam pads ("no straps or fasteners needed") would do the trick, and to make sure they could never shift or fall out, I attached the pads to the shoulders with small pieces of hook-and-loop tape (like Velcro). I fastened the hook portion of the tape to the center of the pads with fabric glue and sewed pieces of the loop tape to corresponding places in the sweaters *(Fig. 181)*. The sweaters fold and store more easily without permanent pads, and I need only one set of pads for all my sweaters.
— *Ruth Neitzel, Merrillville, IN*

PERSONALIZING YOUR WORK
Making designer labels

I use white ⅜-inch satin ribbon and textile paints to make color-coordinated labels for the garments I knit. The paints, nontoxic acrylics, are available at hobby shops in a variety of mixable colors.

Paint a length of ribbon, being sure to

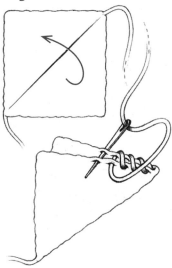

Fig. 180

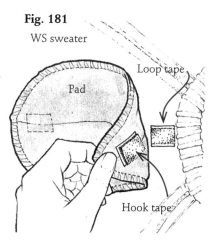

Fig. 181

WS sweater

Loop tape

Pad

Hook tape

saturate the fabric. After it has dried, set the colors with an iron. Then, using a fine-point indelible pen, write your labels. The paint works like sizing and prevents the ink from bleeding. Wash out any excess dye. If you prefer white labels, use white paint.

— *Mary Louise Vidas, Mount Airy, NC*

Fair Isle self-labels

Any machine knitter or determined hand knitter can make a label from the yarn used in the garment. A self-label won't scratch; will have the same color, texture, and care as your work; and makes a great impression. It's fabulous on a one-of-a-kind or limited-edition item.

1. Choose two contrasting yarns of the type used in the piece.

2. Separate the yarns into single plies. If you want a raised effect for the letters, you can use a double ply for them.

3. Knit a monogram or trademark in Fair Isle (1½ by 1 inch).

4. Hand-sew all four sides of the label loosely to the piece.

Fig. 182

100% wool
Hand wash,
cold. Dry flat.

174

5. Attach a fiber-content and care tag to the label, using yarn and a safety pin.

— *Gloria Babiarz, Windsor Locks, CT*

Signing your sweaters

Surface embroidery is an elegant and distinctive way to label knitwear or embellish the outside. I sign my sweaters by writing my name on a piece of cross-stitch canvas or organdy, basting this canvas to the finished knit, and then working over my signature in chain stitch, just catching the surface of the knit through the canvas. When the embroidery is done, I trim away the canvas, slipping out the last threads with tweezers. Cotton floss gives a subtle effect, but silk buttonhole twist stands out a bit more. The chain stitch moves easily with the knit fabric.

— *Jane F. Jull, Friday Harbor, WA*

Nifty gift tag

When giving a handknit sweater as a gift, I cut a sweater-shaped tag from cardboard and punch a hole in one shoulder *(Fig. 182)*. On the tag I write care and cleaning instructions, and fiber content. I wrap a small amount of the sweater's yarn around the middle in case it's needed for mending a hole or seam. Then I tie my custom tag to the sweater with a bow.

— *Lynn Teichman, Lewisburg, PA*

WASHING WOOL AND HANDKNITS

Washing greasy wool

Washing greasy fleece, such as merino, does not have to be difficult and tedious if you know how. There are only two ingredients in the recipe:

- 2 cups pure soap flakes, such as Ivory or Lux (if you can't find flakes, shave a bar of pure soap)

- Denatured alcohol (you can get it at a hardware store)

Slowly pour sufficient alcohol into the soap flakes, stirring constantly, until the mixture is a thick, creamy paste. The mixture will keep for years in a screw-top jar. To wash 5 pounds of greasy wool, put 2 gallons of hot, but not boiling, water into a sink or washtub. You must just be able to keep your hands in the water. Add 2 tablespoons of the creamy mixture and stir until it becomes sudsy. Place the wool in a mesh basket or on a wire screen and dunk it slowly in and out of the water 20 to 30 times. Rinse it in warm, clean water until all the suds are gone. If the wool has any smell, place a small amount of vinegar in the rinse water to remove the odor. Dry the wool on a rack in the sun. Wire netting or a wire platform is ideal.

The wool must dry fairly quickly— within 48 hours—or it could be damaged. The alcohol remains active while it is wet and literally eats up the grease. If the wool remains wet too long, the alcohol may eat the wool fibers as well. If the wool is exceptionally dirty, you may have to wash it a second time after you've rinsed it. Repeat the process with a new solution. Do not simply add more soap to the dirty water.

— *Cyril Lieschke, Henty, NSW, Australia*

Washing cashmere

For years now, I've been washing my wool and cashmere knits in the washing machine. Don't hyperventilate yet. My method simply makes use of the washer's capabilities, assuming you can control some of the functions manually.

Start the washer filling, add your soap or wool detergent, and let mix well. Fold each garment into a neat bundle, as you would when packing for a trip. Distribute these bundles evenly around the washer tub (four is my limit). Let the washer fill until the water level just covers the garments, and turn off the machine. Squish the bundles by hand a bit, then let soak a few minutes. After making sure the items are still in their bundles, set the control to drain the tub and let spin for 10 to 15 seconds. Follow the same procedure for the rinse, allowing the tub to spin just a little longer. Shape and dry flat as usual.

I've never had any stretching or felting using this procedure, and I find it far easier than regular hand-washing.

— *Lynn Roosevelt, Greenville, SC*

Washing cashmere

In an old copy of Italian *Vogue*, I stumbled across a technique for washing cashmere that's never failed to improve my knitwear every time it's washed. I soak the sweater in a cold-water wash for about 5 minutes, squishing it around softly, let the water drain, then squeeze out the sweater. Then I fill the sink with cold water, swish and rinse the sweater, let it drain, and (here's the trick) then I repeat the rinsing 15 times. My hands freeze, but the results are extraordinary. I'm sure that residues from washing are what degrade fine fabrics. I wash silk the same way, but 10 rinses seem to be sufficient.

— *Mary Elliott*

Fluffier handspun yarn

This process, which I came across in *The New Zealand Woolcraft Book* by Constance Jackson and Judith Plowman, goes against everything we've been told about washing wool, but it really makes handspun wool yarn very soft and fluffy. Wash and rinse the skeins of yarn as usual after spinning. Then fill two containers with water—one with the hottest tap water possible and the other with very cold water. Place the wet skeins in the hot water and allow them to absorb the heat for a few minutes. Then plunge them immediately into the cold water. You'll feel the yarn fluffing in your hands.

— *Roseann Charlton, Coraopolis, PA*

Drying fleece and woolens

As a spinner and dyer, I spent a long time searching for an inexpensive, simple way to dry fleece and sweaters in my small apartment. I found my solution at a nearby home center in the form of a light-diffusion grid, normally used under fluorescent-lighting fixtures. Not only is the grid inexpensive, but it's also plastic, so it doesn't rust. It's lightweight, and one grid fits perfectly over my bathtub.

— *Debbie Benzer, Ithaca, NY*

That fishy smell in silk

Pure silk can have a strong, fishy smell when washed, and the odor can sometimes linger after the sweater has dried. It comes from a gum coating, called seracin, that's left on the silk fiber by the silkworm. Most of the gum is removed at the mill during processing by boiling the silk for one to two hours; more comes off during the dyeing process. The final 1 to 2 percent of gum residue is difficult to remove. Generally, the more seracin that's removed during processing, the higher the quality of the finished silk. (And the more that's left on the fiber, the stronger an odor the silk will have.)

The smell from the seracin is strongest when the fiber is wet. The amount of gum (and consequently, the odor) will diminish with repeated washing. I prefer to wash silk, a protein fiber, with shampoo and rinse it with clean water at least three times; adding a hair conditioner to the rinse water fluffs the fiber and gives it fullness. And if you want the silk to have a crunchy feel (called scroop), add a tablespoon of white vinegar to the final rinse. (None of these will improve the smell, however.) After allowing the yarn to garment to dry, you may still notice a slight odor. Most people do not find the smell offensive, once they know that it is.

— *Henry Galler*

Thrift-shop yarn

Thrift shops are often a good source for inexpensive knitting and crochet supplies. When I buy yarn that is dusty and musty, I remove the paper band and, without disturbing the hank as it is wound, I dunk it in cool, sudsy water, then rinse it. I clip one end of the hank to my clothesline in the breeze out of the sun. When one end is dry I reverse it on the line. If crochet cottons have a spot of dirt on the surface of the ball, I use detergent on the spot, leaving the thread on its cardboard cylinder. If the ball becomes wet, I stuff a paper towel inside the hole, and pin the ball to the clothesline.

— *Helen von Ammon, San Francisco, CA*

Softening an itchy sweater

Sheep's wool is in many ways like human hair. After washing a woolen sweater, I rinse it with vinegar to restore the pH balance. If it's itchy, I soften it with a mixture of 2 to 6 tablespoons of hair conditioner and a minimum amount of water, which I spread over the entire garment and between the fibers. After a few minutes, I rinse the sweater thoroughly, towel-dry it, and lay it flat to finish drying.

— *Shelley Karpilow, Berkeley, CA*

Restoring a crocheted tablecloth

To care for a cotton crocheted tablecloth, hand-wash it, using your washing machine as the basin. If the tablecloth has yellowed, presoak it in a peroxy bleach or an enzyme presoak for about half an hour or an hour. Remove it from the washer and fill the machine with hot water and a pure laundry soap. Agitate the water until the soap dissolves, stop the machine, and put the tablecloth back in. Let it soak for another half hour. Rinse it, with no agitation, in hot water and dry it flat, ideally in the sun,

After each use, immediately clean the tablecloth, as just described, using enzyme presoak for protein stains. Never store it dirty; this will attract mold and nasty critters like silverfish. If the tablecloth needs ironing, iron it just before you use it, not before you store it. Store it loosely folded. If you're storing it for any length of time, fold it with acid-free tissue paper (not regular tissue paper) inside the folds and around the cloth.

— *Terry McCormick*

REPAIRING HANDKNITS
Replacement stitching

You can repair a single-stitch sweater hole before it becomes a major project. Gently pull the broken end of the yarn out of the torn stitch. Follow the path of the broken end with replacement yarn threaded on a tapestry needle. Do one loop at a time, replacing all the stitches you wish to repair. I use three-ply Persian tapestry wool (found in most yarn stores), which comes in a variety of colors and can be unraveled. You can also replace a portion of a knitted pattern whose color no longer pleases you with the same technique. No ripping back to the offending color and reknitting.

— *Lynne Vogel, Canyon Beach, OR*

Repairing holes in knits

I'd like to share my techniques for repairing damaged knitwear: First, I never make an even-sided hole. I leave the hole as small as possible. Second, I duplicate-stitch at least two stitches on each side of every row with the second stitch done under the original stitch. And finally, I never use an embroidery hoop for knit repairs. Very few yarns like to be pressed so tightly.

— *Renate Broeker, Memphis, TN*

Taking care of snags and holes

Snags: Many nonknitters are baffled by snags, but these are usually quite easy to repair. If an unbroken loop of yarn sticks out of the knit fabric, it can usually be worked back into the garment. Just think about a row of knit stitches as a series of loops in a strand of yarn, and you will realize that the tight line in the knit fabric is a row of stitches with the fullness yanked out. A little of the extra loop goes back into each of those flat stitches to make them round again. Using a blunt tapestry needle or other pointed tool, carefully pull the fullness back along the tight row, one stitch at a time. Usually, half the extra length goes to the left of the loop and half to the right. To illustrate this process to yourself, gently make a 1-inch snag in one of your sweaters and then repair it. Now any other snags will seem less daunting. I have repaired snags as long as 9 inches in a strong, smooth yarn such as linen, and the damage left not a trace.

Fine silks and smooth, multistranded cottons may be more difficult to repair, because only a part of the yarn may have snagged. This strand is harder to work back in, because it must go back into the yarn as well as into the row of stitches. In thicker double-knit fabrics, it is more difficult to see the sequence of stitches that needs to receive the extra yarn. In either case, first try the technique described above, then pull the remainder of the loop to the wrong side using a crochet or latch hook.

Holes: A real hole in a knit occurs when the yarn is actually broken. Catch and repair these holes early, since small holes are easier to fix and hide than large ones. I repair small holes in fine-gauge knits using matching sewing thread. Sew around the hole near the edge, picking up every loose loop and piercing each broken strand around the edge. Then pull the thread together snugly, sew a couple of stitches in the back to hold it closed, and knot. Practice on cotton underwear and T-shirts with tiny holes.

Prevention is best: It's even better to catch the hole before it happens. Watch for signs of thinness in your favorite garments by holding a single layer of fabric up to the light, which reveals areas of weakness and potential breaks. Repair thin areas using the duplicate stitch in matching but preferably thinner yarn (try separating the plies for a thinner yarn) to reinforce the weak area in horizontal row.

— *Karen Morris*

Keeping stitches secure

To hold a knitted garment securely when picking up dropped stitches or mending a hole, place the section to be worked on a clean hairbrush.

— *Kathleen C. Saxe, Sioux City, IA*

Stealing thread for knit repairs

If you don't have some of the original yarn, you'll have to "steal" the repair yarn from the sweater itself. You need a piece of yarn four times the width of the hole, times the number of missing rows. You can try to borrow the yarn from several locations, with varying amounts of difficulty: At the shoulder seams, there is often a seam allowance of one or more rows that you can unravel. The side seams of many sweaters are joined with their own yarn. Carefully pick open the seams, then resew with another yarn. You can open the armhole seam and steal one to three rows from the top of the sleeve, then resew the seam with another yarn. At the back of the neck, you can open the chain stitches that hold the neckband, remove the excess yarn to the sweater neck, and then resew.

The hardest place from which to steal yarn, but still worth it for a sweater you love, is from the bottom of the sweater body, above the ribbing. Open the lower few inches of the side seam and clip one edge thread two rows above the ribbing. Separate the knit stitch by stitch, remove the amount of yarn you need, and resew. It's best not to press the "stolen" yarn, which could change its thickness.

— *Suzy Hebert*

Repair with felting

When mending small holes in fine-gauge woolen knitwear, it's not always possible to secure the yarn you are using to the frayed edges of the hole. I felt the join slightly instead of overmending with extra stitches. Turn the sweater inside out after making the repair and lay it on a clean, white towel.

Dampen the mended area with a blend of soap and hot water (cautiously proceed with any multicolored garment). Wait until the mixture is thoroughly absorbed into the fibers before rubbing the join gently with a soft toothbrush. This will mat the fibers together.

— *Susan Herrmann, Damascus, OH*

ODDS AND ENDS
Adding ribbing

To add ribbing to a garment that has already been knitted, you can either pick up stitches along the lower edge of the garment (as shown in *Fig. 183),* then knit the ribbing down and bind off, or you can knit the

Fig. 183

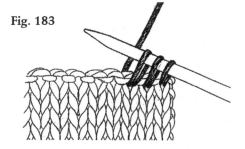

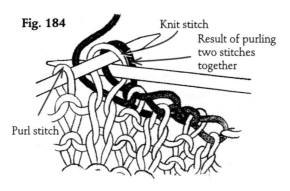

Fig. 184

Knit stitch

Result of purling two stitches together

Purl stitch

ribbing separately, bind off, and sew it onto the garment. Either way, you'll need a stretchy bind-off edge, as is produced by the following technique, which is good on a knit one, purl one rib: Knit two stitches together when the second stitch on the left needle is a knit stitch, as shown in *Fig. 184,* and purl two together when the second stitch on the left needle is a purl stitch. Slip the resulting stitch back to the left needle without twisting, and reposition the right needle behind the yarn to prepare for a purl stitch or in front of the yarn to prepare for a knit stitch. Keeping in the rib pattern, repeat this process until all the stitches are bound off.

Lengthening a finished sweater

If you knit the garment in one piece from the top down and you find you've come up short, simply rip back the bottom ribbing and knit the additional length.

If you knit the garment from the bottom up in separate pieces, open the side seams to 2 inches above the top of the ribbing. Clip a thread on the second row above the ribbing, a few inches away from the knit edge. Undo one row of knitting, catching every stitch from the rows both above and below on two small circular needles, as shown in *Fig. 185.* Knit the desired number of inches on the ribbing section, starting with the second row of the pattern stitch for the body. If there are cables or an intricate pattern stitch, make sure that you stop knitting one row short of where the pattern of the top piece begins. Graft the newly lengthened ribbing section to the old body of the sweater with Kitchener stitch, joining knit stitches as knits and purl stitches as purls.

If you knit the body in a pattern stitch, you must knit up from the ribbing instead of down from the body section. If you were to knit down, picking up the bottom loop of the knitted stitches, the knitting of the

Fig. 185

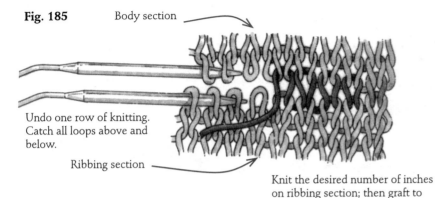

Body section

Undo one row of knitting.
Catch all loops above and
below.

Ribbing section

Knit the desired number of inches
on ribbing section; then graft to
body section.

bottom section would be a half loop off the top section's knitting, and the pattern would not align.

Lengthening a sweater is easier said than done when a pattern stitch is involved or if you have never before faced the trauma of cutting open a piece of knitting. The best solution is prevention. Before beginning underarm shaping, hold the body piece up to the wearer and assess the length. These few minutes of double-checking can prevent a lot of grief.

— *Maggie Righetti*

Zippers in knits

A zipper should be sewn to a knit very carefully by hand. A knit garment has a lot of give, whereas a zipper tape has none, so the spacing of the knit fabric along the zipper tape must be precisely adjusted. Open the zipper and pin it to the garment with many pins. Be sure the knitting is neither stretched nor compressed and that corresponding sides match exactly. This is especially important if there are horizontal stripes or other patterns. Sew on the wrong side with small, close stitches. Catch just the backs of the knit stitches with the needle so the right side doesn't dimple.

— *Barbara Walker*

ABBREVIATIONS

ch	Chain		p2tog-b	Purl two together through the back loops
cn	Cable needle		psso	Pass slipped stitch over
dc	Double crochet		RHN	Right-hand needle
dec	Decrease		RS	Right side
hdc	Half double crochet		sc	Single crochet
inc	Increase		sl	Slip
k	Knit		ssk	Slip, slip, knit
k2tog	Knit two together		st(s)	Stitch(es)
k-2tog-b	Knit two together through the back loops		St st	Stockinette stitch
kwise	Knitwise		tog	Together
LHN	Left-hand needle		tr	Treble crochet
lp	Loop		WS	Wrong side
p	Purl		wyib	With yarn in back
pwise	Purlwise		wyif	With yarn in front
p2tog	Purl two together		yo	Yarn over

INDEX

Note: **Bold** page numbers indicate that an illustration is included, and *italicized* page numbers indicate that a table is included. (When only one number of a page range is **bold** or *italicized*, an illustration or table is located on one or more of the pages.)

A

Acrylic yarn, 3–4
Alpaca yarn, 4–5
Aran sweaters, 110
Armholes, 102–3
    See also Steeks

B

Baseball stitches, **168**
Binding off, **50**–57, **141**–42
Blocking, 172
Bobbins, **78**–80
Bobbles, **36**
Booties, designing, **112**–13
Buttonholes, **22, 90**–95, 152–54

C

Calculating stitches, 84–85
Cardigan front bands, 88–90
Care, **175**–78
Carpal tunnel syndrome, 59–60
Casting on, **19–22,** 24–25, **137**–39
Center-pull balls, **8–9**
Chenille yarn, 3
Children. *See* Knitting for kids
Circular knitting, *24–31*
Coils, knitting, 144–145
Color blending, 5, 16–17, **73**–76,
    154, 171
    See also Stranded knitting
Conversions. *See* Stitch equivalents
Cord makers, **115**–116
Corrugating ribs, 39
Counting rows, 121, 158

Crochet techniques, **150**–54,
Cuffs, 99

D

Decreases, **40**–46, **140**
Discomfort, 59–60, 157
Dorset buttons, 96–**97**
Duplicate stitches, **72–73**

E

Edges, 155, **170**–171
Elastic ribbing, 39–39
Elastic thread, 11
Elongated stitches, 34–**35**

F

Facings, 109
Fair Isle, 65–**67**, 121–22
Fingering yarn, 6
First row, knitting, 21
Fringe, **171**

G

Gauge, 83–85
Grafting, **164**–66

H

Hand knitting, 119
   See also specific technique
Hand-washing, 175–78

I

Increases, **40**–46, **140**, **150–51**
Intarsia knitting, **67**–73
Isolation lace, 141

J

Joining yarn, 26–27, **123**–24, 167–68

K

Kids. *See* Knitting for kids
Kitchener stitches, **164**
Knit stitches, **32**–34
Knitting backward, **61**
Knitting for kids, *86–88,* 94, 99

L

Labels, making, 173–**75**
Left-handed knitting, **22**–24, 80
Leftover yarn, **12**–16
Leftward knitting, **60**–61
Lengthening sweaters, 182–**83**

M

Machine knitting, **140–144**
   See also specific technique
Mattress stitches, 166–**67**
Measuring, 6–7
Multicolor knitting. *See* Color
      blending; Stranded knitting
Muslins, 85

N

Necklines, **102**–5, 142–**44**
Needle tips, 119–20
NeedleMaster™, 141

P

Pain, 59–60, 157
Patterns, 85, 120–23, 145
Picking up stitches, **57–59**, 102–**105**
Pilling, 17